Praise for

"Thomas Dismukes is fantastic! A Southern boy with a Southern accent that's fun, funny, and entertaining with a purpose."

—Lynn Skeele-Flynn
Senior Vice-President, YMCA

"Phenomenal! When [Thomas] speaks, it's captivating."

—Stephanie Trippeer
Staples

"A strong message that was delivered in a light and entertaining manner. You've boosted the spirits of our staff and faculty!"

—Dr. Arthur Kirk
President, Saint Leo University

"Thomas Dismukes is GREAT! We all laughed so hard we cried."

—Danny Glossup
Dairy Farmers of America

"One of the most talented and sincere speakers I have ever met."

—Ramona Huckstep
Missouri Department of Natural Resources

"Thomas, you're a gold mine!"

—YPO Leysin, Switzerland

"Even as adults, we need to be reminded of what true success really entails and how important it is for us to have that encouragement and hope in our lives, and [Thomas] was able to do that. The lessons [Thomas] taught were right in line with what Relay for Life really stands for, giving hope and encouragement to others, even when there are many roadblocks and hurdles to overcome."

—Sherry Freeman
American Cancer Society; Relay for Life

"You and your chin are amazing!"

—Jeanne White
Red Hat Society, South Carolina Queen's Council

"[Thomas's] stories and messages were thought provoking and relevant."

—Ray Patrick
Missouri Association of Rural Education

"[Thomas] kept the audience spellbound!"

—Chick-fil-A

"[Thomas's] message was perfect, and the humor even better!"

—Micki Kidder
University of Notre Dame

"How can you be so young with this many stories, but wise enough to decipher such powerful principles? Phenomenal!"

—Louisiana Cable & Telecommunications

# A LEADER'S FOCUS

To: Mary,

All the best
and nothing less than success!

Thomas

THOMAS DISMUKES
INTERNATIONAL MOTIVATIONAL STORYTELLER:
HUMORIST, AND ADVENTURER

# A LEADER'S FOCUS

FINDING THE BALANCE
THAT DETERMINES PERSONAL AND
PROFESSIONAL SUCCESS

Pentastic

STORIES THAT TELL

*TELLING STORIES THAT EQUIP TODAY'S LEADERS.*

## Contact Thomas
Book Thomas for your corporate event
and learn more at:
www.ThomasDismukes.com

Published in York, SC by Pentastic Publishing.

Cover design by Red Panda Productions

**Library of Congress Cataloging-in-Publication Data**
Dismukes, Thomas,
    A leader's focus : finding the balance that determines personal and professional success/ Thomas Dismukes

        p. cm
    ISBN 978-0-9882063-0-4 (pbk.)
1. Leadership- Success-  2. Conduct of life- Christian life  3. Motivational stories -Non-fiction  I. Title
Manufactured in the United States of America

This story was written for our children:
Hudson – the Conscientious Leader
Colette – the Exploring Spirit
Ellie – the Affectionate Joy
Rasmine – the Kindhearted Knower
Womb Baby – the Quiver is Full


And dedicated first to:
Kimberly, my beloved bride. Your strength of
character astounds me.
You are water to a wilting plant. I like you.


And second, to:
Those who still believe they can accomplish the
dreams of their youthful spirit.

# Contents

# Acknowledgments

Philip Carper: Our website and computer genius. A work horse, dreamer, doer, and more importantly, a friend. Your work ethic, encouragement, and passion inspire ME.

Elbert "Beaver" Charpie: You were there at the genesis and have given me invaluable revelation. Your wisdom and guidance have been in the center of it all.

Paige Hardcastle: Your latent talent amazes me. The generosity of your time and limitless desire to learn and share knowledge is contagious.

Christina Huffines: Absolutely, the best editor in the world. A true talent and gift. Your ability to see what others do not astonishes me. You have made it fun.

# Foreword

It was way too wobbly. If it fell, the shattered glass would end the game and my hope to break the record. But what do you expect when you stack 95 pint-size glasses inside themselves? Collectively the glasses weighed more than 100 pounds, so when I put the wobbling tower on my chin, I could feel parts of my jaw stretch and pull. Standing on home plate during the seventh-inning stretch, I had come to terms I would most likely fail in front of the curious baseball fans. Whoever said breaking a world record would be easy?

Of all the random "gifts" and talents that can possibly be bestowed, mine is the ability to balance most anything on my chin. I discovered and developed this talent as a child, when I would balance macaroni boxes and canned goods on the kitchen floor as my mom cooked. Balancing objects on the floor evolved to mops and brooms on my finger, then ladders, sailboats, and teenagers on my chin. It was pretty much a useless talent. People always smiled and were amazed, a reaction similar to the joy of seeing a dozen clowns crawl out of a Little Tikes push car. But there I was, June 30, 2005, attempting to break the world record by balancing 95 pint-size glasses on my chin for more than 10.6 seconds.

17.8 seconds later, it was over. My jaw was dislocated and my chin was cut, but I had just broken a world record. People smiled and cheered, but the fame was short lived. The seventh-inning stretch was over and the umpire wanted to "Play ball!"

Balancing things on my chin and breaking a world record wasn't the most exciting thing I had done in my life, only one of many things I had yet to find a reason or meaning behind. Years ago, I learned the principle that everything happens for a reason. Good, bad, and ugly, you can learn from everything in life. There is an old saying that experience is learning from your mistakes and wisdom is learning from someone else's mistakes. Unfortunately, only some of us learn from other people's mistakes; the rest of us have to be the other people.

"God looks after children and idiots," and I've always fallen into one of those categories. In my relatively short-lived life, I've skinned skunks in space suits and lassoed wild beavers. I've slept in the Sistine Chapel, a dumpster in England, and train stations in Czechoslovakia. I've ridden in rodeos, raised copperheads, and discovered a lost tomb in Scotland. I had the joy of walking in the Alps barefoot and exploring the Arctic Circle. I have truly been blessed to meet people from all walks of life: professional athletes, Olympians, military officers, CEO's, U.S. public officials, billionaires, and beggars. I've dug into the minds of children and have heard the wisdom of the elderly's last dying words.

It is through all of their wisdom, leadership, or lack thereof that I gather meaning that has greatly influenced my life and the lives of countless others. It is the inexplicable pursuit of a life in balance. A life not of indecision and inconsistency, but one of peace, purpose, and priority. We all strive to balance our personal and professional lives, to be remembered and to live a life of significance. It is this balance and significance that one can find while mastering "a leader's focus."

One of the greatest gifts a story can give is a lesson from a life you do not have to live. Nestled within each triumphant or disastrous event of this book lies a story that tells a fundamental principle. Learning these principles helps provide the foundation for a healthy, balanced, and successful life. More often than not, the problems and struggles we endure are direct results of improper focus and ill-placed priorities. When our focus is in proper balance, the result is peace, contentment, peak performance, and a defining purpose.

Please do not take this comment as braggado-cios, but I am blessed with a beautiful bride, five wonderful children, financial peace, contentment, and the joy of doing what I love to do. The reason I am at this place in my life is not because of superior intelligence or being raised in an affluent family. I made the top 90 percent of my class possible, and the only silver spoons I knew of was a show with Rick Schroder. Growing up I thought everyone had six children and lived in a two-bedroom house.

Early in my life, I was blessed to have an affinity towards people who were in their last few years of life. Living off the understanding that everyone is my superior, because I can learn something from them, I knew if I asked the right questions, the amount of wisdom these people could bestow upon me would be limitless. A few of my favorite questions to ask were, What is something you wish you knew when you were my age? What would you do differently or do more of, if you could do it all over? Any words of advice, wisdom, or suggestions for me? If you had a minute left to live, what would you want the world to know? I was amazed to discover that so many people experienced the same types of problems and expressed similar advice to avoid those problems. It would be asinine to not take that wisdom and apply it to my life to avoid the problems so many people repeat generation after generation.

A Leader's FOCUS is a culmination of that wisdom I have gathered over the years. The wisest man in history, King Solomon, once wrote, "There is nothing new under the sun." Unfortunately, each generation must relearn these core leadership principles, master them, and then pass them along to the next generation. If we are fortunate and wise enough to learn and follow these principles at an early age, the effects can be profound over a lifetime.

Don't get me wrong—I don't claim to know everything, and this isn't a cure-all book. I'm still young, dumb, and in love, but I've discovered that what seems like common sense is not common practice. You may already know and encourage these principles, but knowing and doing are two entirely different things. A Leader's FOCUS is not for the lazy because it requires immediate and continual action.

Instead, A Leader's FOCUS is for the few who want peace, purpose, and a life in balance—those who desire to be leaders in all areas of life. This is a simple yet challenging book for business executives, sales managers, support staff, teachers and students, personnel workers, preachers, husbands and wives, fathers and mothers—everyone whose intention is to challenge men and women to superior accomplishments. If you are determined to have a leader's focus, use this book as a platform for telling your story and adventuring toward your highest possibilities.

It's not easy to have a focused and balanced life; the alternative, in fact, is easier: a wrecked marriage, spoiled children, dead-end jobs, poor relationships, and a lack of hope and fulfillment. Beginning now, let us live a life of harmony and significance. Let us live A Leader's FOCUS.

# FIRST THINGS FIRST

## BUCKTOOTH

The art of taxidermy has always fascinated me. If a craftsman preserves and mounts a hide properly, the animal looks real, almost frozen in time. Sure, it takes talent and know-how . . . but truly, how hard could it be? If given the chance, I figured I could do it with ease!

During my college career at Clemson University, I lived on Starkey Pig Farm. The pig odor was a bit pungent, and the property was not necessarily a romantic place to bring a date, but the rent was cheap. I was driving home to the farm one day when I passed a freshly killed beaver beside the road. It was a beauty, in pristine shape! Living by the attitude of "How often do you get to skin a beaver?" I slammed on the breaks and tossed the specimen onto the bed of Ole Bessie. (Ole Bessie was my '76 Chevy step-side pickup truck, with more rust than frame and an unplanted tree growing in the back of her wooden bed. She was half mobile and half motel. She got about ten miles to the gallon, and when I hit a mud puddle, my feet got wet. The ladies loved Ole Bess because she had "personality," but like her rusty frame, I digress.)

I took my prize home with great anticipation, and visions of a masterfully mounted beaver danced in my head. I could see it as clear as day. It would be sitting up on its hind legs, its left paw outstretched holding a bowl full of candy, with the other hand raised high, waving to all who came in the door. With an enormous smile, it would be the greeter to my humble abode. I would call the creation "Bucktooth."

I couldn't wait to start my project! I went to the store and bought wooden dowels, wire, pillow stuffing (antibiotic of course . . . I wanted to be sanitary), a Styrofoam ball, and two black marbles. I then hurried home and began to skin the future Bucktooth. Once the skin was removed, I washed it off with water and began to construct the internal framework out of the wire and dowels. I measured its head and molded the Styrofoam and then glued the marble eyes in place. The masterpiece was coming together perfectly. Next, working my way from the bottom up, I wrapped the wet skin around the frame, packed in the pillow stuffing, and sewed it shut. I used my roommate's hair dryer and comb to tease Bucktooth's hair and then placed him on the kitchen counter to welcome visitors. He was finished! In fewer than two hours a carcass on the side of the road had been transformed into a beautiful, smiling, candy-dish-holding, high-fiving stuffed beaver named Bucktooth. I almost cried I was so proud of myself.

A week went by and Bucktooth kept on smiling, waving, and handing out candy. His smile wasn't quite as big as it had been, but he still looked great! It was about two weeks after Bucktooth's "birth" that I noticed an odd smell in the house. With a pig farm only 100 feet away, strange and putrid odors were not uncommon, so I thought nothing of it. But I did notice that Bucktooth's face was sagging a bit. He just didn't seem to have that "fresh" look to him anymore. Some three weeks passed, and the odor became much stronger with a consistent hint of decay. It was about that time when I was taking candy from Bucktooth that I noticed dozens of tiny white dots all over his face. On closer inspection I discovered they were not dots of dust or even beaver dandruff, but rather hundreds of hungry maggots. Needless to say, I didn't swallow the candy. No wonder the friendly smile had turned into a depressing frown, and the welcoming waving paw had . . . disappeared! It had collapsed inward from nearly rotting away! In disgust I reached out and grabbed Bucktooth's body, but when I did, my hands, along with the hair I was gripping, slipped off the hide. The entire body was rotten!

In my haste to mount the beaver I didn't take the proper steps necessary to preserve the hide. I didn't salt or tan it—it went straight from the animal to the artificial body. My preservation efforts were a total waste and totally made me sick! We couldn't get the rancid stench out of the place for a month. I was disappointed. But in the end, a couple of valuable lessons were learned. For one . . . Don't ever do that again!

Billy Graham once said, "Until a person gets his priorities in life straight, everything else is going to be out of order." There is truly a proper and logical order we should have for our lives. Establishing this order to maintain our priorities is the keystone of A Leader's FOCUS. Unfortunately, our lives can often reflect the story of Bucktooth: We have plans and dreams, but in our haste and ignorance we skip steps and put our priorities out of order. We see people who look "successful" on the outside, but if we look closer into their lives, they are hurting and decaying on the inside.

If you will, please indulge me in this simple object lesson. If you complete these steps in the proper order, I will "telepathetically" read your mind, even through the pages of this book.

Step 1:

Think of any three-digit number. However, the number cannot repeat all digits (e.g., 222, 999) or be a mirror image of itself (575, 121). _____ For my example I will use *123*.

Step 2:

Now reverse your number. _____ *321*

Step 3:

Subtract the smaller number from the larger number in the previous steps. (If you now have a two digit number, add a 0 at the end of the number.) _____ *321-123 = 198*

Step 4:

Reverse the answer from Step 3. _____ *891*

Step 5:

Finally, add the answers from Step 3 and Step 4. _____ *198 + 891*

I predict your answer to be . . . alla . . . wha . . . la . . . peanut butter . . . . 1089. (If you didn't get that number, go back and recheck your arithmetic.)

Like yourself, your number was uniquely made. The process in achieving this number is just as predictable as physical and philosophical laws like gravity and reaping what you sow: If you follow the correct steps, there is an expected outcome. Similarly, there are correct steps or principles to follow and incorporate into your life. Once they are established, the outcome is peace, joy, fruitfulness, contentment, and a life of significance.

# The Main Thing

Bestselling author John C. Maxwell often says, "Everything rises and falls on leadership." I'll also add that leadership rises and falls with one's priorities. There is no doubt in my mind there are set priorities for life that will keep us in check and balance. Over the years, I've found that if these priorities are built on a solid-rock foundation, relationships and careers will withstand the storms that will most assuredly pound our shores. How can you expect to perform at the highest levels at work when our personal lives are unsatisfactory? Bill Ames, Director of Auto Shows for General Motors explains, "A person whose marriage is not the best, whose communication with his children is on shaky ground, who has no great hope for a brighter future and is not certain that he is making a difference anyway…this person cannot possibly be as effective or productive a member of the team as he could be. And frankly, no amount of specific training about "how to sell" or "how to lead" is going to change that." If you want to have a good focus in life, a good balance between your professional and personal life, keep First Things First. First Things First is the foundation for the rest of this book. Do not underestimate the importance and power of this step—it is so easy to say but often so hard to do.

I once struggled over a decision to do something that would be either best for my family or best for my job. I happened to mention the issue to a friend of mine. Without hesitation, he said, "It's simple, really: keep the main thing, the main thing." That simple yet profound advice made my decision simple and, in the end, made a world of difference in my relationship with my family. The response to this simple statement from countless others has been staggeringly similar.

Can it be done? Can you have a financially successful life and have a successful and productive family? Of course you can! The "how to" is pretty simple. It's the "must do" that's hard. We have to work hard to support our families. We want nice things and the ability to go to nice places, but healthy balance regarding family and work is a tipping point that many struggle with. Years ago, I spoke to an insurance company in New Hampshire. Afterward, I had a few minutes to speak with the CEO. In a revealing moment he told me that he had worked hard all his life. Materially, he had everything he wanted. With tears in his eyes he told me, "Thomas, I'm a multi-millionaire. I truly have everything I really want and need in life . . . except for one thing. I would trade my entire fortune away if I could just have a better relationship with my wife. We started off with a little more than $400 in our bank account when we were married. We had nothing, but looking back, we had more than we do now. I would give my fortune away if my children even knew who I was. Don't get me wrong, Thomas, all our 'toys' are nice . . . but I question now, at what cost?" Indeed, this man had the world but lost his family. What's the point if you win in business but lose in life?

Similarly, I had the opportunity to speak to a group of very affluent teenagers in Switzerland. All the kids were from families of dignitaries, presidents and CEO's, ambassadors, and even a few were royalty. They were all great kids. (I've found that kids are kids no matter where you are in the world.) Knowing their parents' financial background, I asked the students what they wanted most in life. Every material thing was easily obtainable to them. Most, if not all, had personal assistants and housekeepers, and many of the kids did not speak to their parents directly but through "family planners." So I was not surprised to hear that what they wanted most in life was to have more devoted time with their parents.

How do you balance personal and professional life? Take a moment, if you will, to write down your priorities. What or who is the main thing in your life? That's your "First Things First." Then list your second through fifth priorities. You may already have your priorities in place, but do you have them in practice?

1._____

2._____

3._____

4._____

5._____

Speaking from personal experience and countless testimonies, I've listed the following priorities of mine and ones I've found to be shared by that rare breed of those who have lived successful lives of significance.

# Priorities of A Leader's FOCUS

Priority #1: Your relationship with God
(Mark 12:30, Proverbs 3:5-6)

First Things First in my life is my daily walk and relationship with Jesus Christ. As a Christian, I ensure that my relationship with Christ comes before all other relationships. Through God's grace, a growing faith is a lifetime of obedience and reflection. My relationship with God gives me purpose, hope, joy, and peace and makes me a better husband, father, friend, and employer. There is no doubt in my mind

God exists and truly wants a day-to-day relationship with the ones He created.

It was Bill Cosby who often disciplined his children with the saying, "I brought you in this world, and I can take you out!" In that same regard (though less threatening), the Creator of this universe has given me the ability to live and breathe each day; He brought me in this world, and eventually He'll take me out. A daily walk with God not only gives us wisdom and understanding ("No eye has seen, no ear has heard, no mind has conceived what God has prepared for those who love Him"—1 Corinthians 2:9), but it also keeps us humbled and grounded. If you master the remaining principles in this book and find your life still lacking, I urge you to reevaluate this relationship.

"It's my world and you live in it" is the mantra of the weak and those who are searching for purpose. The world does not revolve around you. You are replaceable. You are dispensable. Don't get me wrong; you are special, a one-of-a-kind individual with unique abilities, talents, skills, and passions. We are here for a reason. But to be so narcissistic as to think the world will stop turning without you is foolish. A relationship with God helps us see the bigger picture. Though I do not understand the mind of God, I do seek His wisdom and plan for my life. I understand my time on earth is temporal and it is my responsibility to be intentional and fruitful in my thoughts and actions so as to best live according to His will.

## Priority #2: Your relationship with your spouse
(Ephesians 5:21-33)

"If momma ain't happy, ain't nobody happy." Your relationship with your spouse is the first earthly priority for a balanced life. Healthy relationships take time and quite a bit of work to build. We commit so much time and energy to a job that we will eventually retire from yet so little to a marital relationship that can last a lifetime. You can't be a good father or mother unless you're a good husband or wife first. From a child's perspective, as long as mom and dad are great, life is great.

If you are single, focus on building your relationship with your parents or guardian and other family members.

## Priority #3: Your relationship with your children
(Proverbs 22:6)

Everything we have is on loan. We came into this world with nothing and we'll leave with the same. If we are blessed to have children, we are responsible for teaching and training them to respect others, take personal responsibility for their actions, and contribute to the betterment of the family, community, and country through use of their unique talents and hard work. We raise our children to let them go because they, too, are on loan. Keeping a personal balance requires having a strong and loving relationship with your children.

This relationship is about quantity and quality. Some of my fondest memories growing up are the times I had playing with my mother and father. Whether it was passing ball and wrestling with my dad or reading and cooking with my mom, my parents planted "I-love-you seeds" by spending time with me, encouraging me, listening to me, and taking advantage of teachable moments. My parents expected their children to obey, to work, and to take responsibility for their actions. "No Work, No Pay! No Work, No Play!" my mother would often say. They were never short on healthy discipline and often allowed natural consequences to be the punishment. But there was never a doubt in our minds that Mom and Dad loved us and wanted what was best for us. As we were still sniffling and snotting over ourselves from a spanking, they would sit us on their laps and gently explain what we did wrong. They were consistent in their discipline and love for us.

The only time I sing is in the shower and to my children as they go to bed. As my children have grown, I've written a song that helps remind me of my focus on them. It's an endearing (if not cheesy) little song, but it's a simple reminder to keep First

Things First.

## "Do You Know My Name?"

Hello, little baby. Do you know my name?
I've not seen you in a long long time and I've never
been the same.
I know I should have been there, I even said I would.
I never dreamed I should have said, I wish I could.
I'd come home late every day, trying to make that
extra dime.
How'd I know all my little things would cause me to
miss your bedtime?

Hello, little girl. Do you know my name?
I've not seen you in a long long time and I've never
been the same.
You asked me if I'd sit awhile and have a tea party.
Why did I ever say, "Oh, we'll see"?
I'd come home late every day, trying to help that
extra one.
How I'd know their needy list would never ever get
done?

Hello, little boy. Do you know my name?
I've not seen you in a long long time and I've never
been the same.
You asked me if I'd come out and pass a ball or two.
What could I've possibly done, to say I've got too
many things to do?
I'd come home late every day, trying to make that
extra dime.

How'd I know all my little toys would cause me to
miss your playtime?

Hello, little children, will you forgive me?
I've finally figured out how to spell love . . .
it's T-I-M-E.

## Priority #4: Your relationships with family members
(1 Peter 4:10-11)

Next to our spouses and children are our other family members. I guess I have an abnormal family in that my parents are still married, I have a great relationship with my five other siblings, and I love my aunts, uncles, and cousins. Sure, we have had our problems over the years, but things have been dealt with and resolved. How foolish and sad it is to harbor grudges and regrets for years. My family is a leg I can lean on. This foundation has been built on Christ, sincere love, trust, service, communication, humor, honesty, and pride in who we are. If you don't have a healthy relationship with family members, then get moving and start turning in that direction now. Remember, a ship moving is a lot easier to turn than one standing still.

## Priority #5: Your relationships with a wise council of friends.
(Proverbs 11:14, 12:15)

A true friend is someone that is genuinely happy for your success. It's important to cultivate relationships with a circle of friends who will help keep you accountable. Your relationships, best limited to eight or fewer close friends, should be strong enough that your friends can stop you from doing something wrong or give you a swift kick in the pants to get you going. Iron sharpens iron. Your thoughts, habits, actions, character, and beliefs become the average of the top five friends you hang out with. I have even seen studies that show your income will become the average of the top five friends you associate with. There is a lot of truth behind the saying that birds of a feather flock together.

Priority #6: Your career.

If you have taken care of the top five priorities, your career will be more fulfilling and purposeful. People often take a job just because they need the money, not taking into consideration how it fits with their unique talents and passions. Think of how much happier people would be if they put the time, effort, and work into finding a job that they love. If you never want to work another day in your life because you love what you do, find a career that meets these three criteria:

1. A career you are passionate about. It will not be a bed of roses all the time, but it's a career you will enjoy. Some people may even call it their calling. You would be amazed and saddened how few people

can say this about their job. In fact, a recent study by Forbes magazine stated that 87.5 percent of Americans hate their jobs and 74 percent of people would quit their jobs today, or are actively searching for another.

2. A career you are talented at. We all have genuine, unique talents. Yes, you do have unique talents! For example, ask yourself, What three things happened today or this week that made it "a good day" or "good week"? Now go deeper and find out why they happened. What did you do or say to help make that possible? There are countless careers that utilize those specific skills.

3. A career you can make money in. You have to support yourself and your family. A government handout is not a career. It takes money to go and do the things you need and want to do with the ones you love. Financial freedom is a byproduct of successfully meeting the first two criteria. How much money you earn is in direct proportion to the amount of people you serve, the amount of risk you take, and the value of service you provide.

All three of these criteria must be met to maximize your chances of finding contentment and purpose in your career. You may be passionate about and talented at making mud pies, but you can't make money in it. (On second thought, if you can sell a potato chip that looks like Elvis for $10,000, maybe you can make money in mud-pie masterpieces.) If you are passionate about a singing career, you can certainly have the potential to make money in the industry, but if you have no talent—well, the preliminary contestants on American Idol prove that point. Finally, you may be good at what you do and are thus making good money, but if you wake up Monday morning stressing out because you hate your job, you are only helping the careers in family counseling, the sale of antidepressants, and gravediggers.

Let me close out First Things First by working backwards. Eventually, no matter how great or bad your job is, you'll stop working. You'll either have a physical or mental problem that keeps you from working, or you'll retire, get laid off, sell the company, or be too old to effectively manage it. There will be a point when the energy and identity you put into your career will no longer matter. As depressing as it is, we are expendable and disposable; it is the foolish and immature who believe, "This is my world and you live in it." My father shocked me into seeing this reality as a teenager, when I was working my way through college driving forklifts for the company he worked for. In my mind I was the absolute best forklift driver who was ever employed. I was efficiently fast but safe. I always came in early and left late. Other employees even told me to stop working so hard because it made them look bad. I naively worried that this multibillion dollar company might stumble or lose stock value once I left for school.

I shared with my father my deep concerns regarding the welfare of his company. I was expecting my father to say, "Yes, son, it will be hard, but eventually we'll make it out of this tremendous loss." To my chagrin, my father simply scoffed and said, "Son, you'll be replaced tomorrow." I kid you not—my simple teenage mindset of "the world revolves around me and is dependent on me" was crushed. The thought of not being wanted or needed bothered me for quite a while. It's strange, I see those same emotions coming from people who retire after 30 years of service or being laid off from companies they "gave everything" to.

There is an ancient proverb that says, "When you feel you are irreplaceable, stick your fist in a bucket of water and pull it out. As fast as the water replaces the void where your hand once was, is as fast as you too will be replaced." That's the way life is. Life is so short. Why would you not do what you love to do?

Eventually your friends and family will move or pass away. If you are blessed to have the responsibility of raising children, they, too, will fly away to start lives of their own. Your spouse, as heartbreaking as it is to think, will eventually leave you through death as well ("Till death do us part"). So now, the only things left are you, the choices you have made, the character you have left behind, and the relationship you have or do not have with your Maker.

Over the years, I have had the honor to spend time with people who were moments or days away from death. Some had lived long, healthy lives, while some had suffered badly from illnesses that took over their teenage bodies. The very special moments I had with those wonderful lives will forever be a part of me. One thing I asked many was what it felt like to be close to death. What would they do differently, or more of, if they could live life over? Fewer than 12 hours before his death, my teenage friend Ricky Gammage told me, "Life is truly a gift. Enjoy each precious moment you have with the ones you love." Those wise and loving words were echoed by countless others. Many have told me they wished they had spent more time with their families. They've laughed at the silly things they had harbored for years against their friends or family members. They wished they had traveled more, read the Bible more, laughed more. With all those people, I never once heard— not even a hint—someone say they wished they had spent more time at the office.

My friends, things are rarely what they seem to be. A word of warning: expect surprises in life. We have to work to provide the essentials of life and things that give us pleasure, although temporary.

However, there are spiritual, emotional, and physical priorities that, if we keep in proper order and perspective, can bring about a life with little regret and great peace.

Most would agree with the above priorities; however, what we say are our priorities and what we do as priorities are sometimes entirely different things. To say keeping these priorities is easy would be foolish. On the contrary, it's hard. Everything around us focuses on what's in it for me, me, me? Our culture promotes self-reliance, self-esteem, and selfishness: "I want it now, because I deserve it!" We are quick to claim our rights and slow to claim responsibility. It's hard not to fall into the trap of self-absorption, pride, mediocrity, dependency, and fear. There is no doubt that if you set the standards of A Leader's FOCUS for your life, you will find peace, confidence, and balance in everything you do.

# The Night of King Anaboa

It was one of those ideas that seems too simple to actually work, much less fool people. The idea originated with my younger brother, Samuel, and his counterpart cousin, Benjamin. Individually they were decently smart young boys, but put the two together, and they synergistically turned into a diabolical genius. It was not unusual to find evidence of their weekend pastimes scattered all throughout the community. An example of their escapades was when one would lie down on the road in jumping-jack position, while the other would spray-paint around him, giving the impression that only moments earlier a detective had traced around a victim's dead body. For a couple of weeks, our county was an art gallery of "murder scenes." To this day I don't believe the real-estate value has recovered its significant loss due to the high "murder" rate in the area.

Regardless of the origin, once the new and devious idea reached the home front, we all added our own individual flare to the masterpiece. All we needed was an inner tube out of Mom's bike, gravel out of the aquarium, spray paint, fingernail polish, and Dad's good fishing rod. The design was actually quite simple, yet interwoven throughout its plan was the psychological manipulation of every human's innate fear. The fear . . . of snakes.

We pulled the rubber inner tube out of Mom's bike and cut it so that it would relax to make a six-foot-long tube. We then tied off an end and filled the tube with gravel and sand. Any remaining space we packed with Dad's socks. We closed up our little package of mayhem by tying the other end and attached it to Dad's favorite fishing pole. (We spared no expense!) Adding the final extra touch, we spray-painted the tube and even glued on glitter to make it appear more exotic. In regular daylight it looked like a malformed, puffed up, glittery, painted inner tube with its ends tied. However, in the dark, with a little movement, a little light, the art of surprise, and a lot of built-up hatred and an intense phobia of reptiles, it evolved into a three- inch-thick, six-foot-long cross between an anaconda, a boa constrictor, and a king snake. We reverently and affectionately hailed it "King Anaboa!"

We lived on a two-lane road that was respectively busy but not dangerous. In the right position, one of us could see a car coming from up or down the road and have just enough time to yell, "Car! Man your stations!" With the fishing rod in hand, one person would lay low in the grass 100 feet away, while someone on the road would coil the "snake" into a nice "striking" pose. The fishing pole guy would gently take the slack out of the line and then wait for the cue. The tension would build until the magic word came: "Car!" When the headlights crested the hill, everyone would hide to prepare themselves. Then as the car approached, the one with the fishing rod would hoist the rod to the left then jerk it far to the right as he reeled the line in. This movement would transform an ordinary inner tube into King Anaboa! From the driver's perspective, it would appear that an enormous snake, which had been startled by their car, was now trying to escape for the safety of the ditch.

Like puppeteers we were able to make King Anaboa slither, roll, and even skip! Once we activated the snake, it was amazing to watch people's reactions. At least nine out of ten cars would position their tires to run over the snake. Many would run over it, scream obscenities, and then actually back up several times to run over the snake again! We often heard the passengers scream to the driver, "Kill it! Kill it!" I can still remember a yellow Camaro circling the block six times to kill the snake! I guess he didn't think it was strange that each time he circled around, the snake would return to its coiled position just to slide away again. Eventually he must have realized he was being tricked or was content to know he would never kill a snake that he had run over half a dozen times.

Apparently, word of the snake spread quickly. When we would take a break, people would drive by and warn us, "Watch out, there's a big snake around here!" To push the envelope a little further, Phillipp, my older brother, dragged the inner tube to the edge of the ditch and began to beat it with a stick while people drove by. Once again, more screams of terror: "Ahh! Look at that big snake!" People would actually get out of their cars to help beat the snake or just to watch the spectacle. I remember one guy even offered his gun. I think we probably would have shot it to add to the drama, but we figured Mom wouldn't like her bicycle tube ruined.

Unfortunately, the fun for the evening came to a quick and dramatic stop. Ben discovered if he hung the line over a tree limb, he could make King Anaboa jump up and spin several feet off the road. The first approaching car, however, came quicker than he had anticipated, so when he caused the snake to jump, the fishing line caught onto the car's bumper. We were all so focused on seeing the first ever snake pirouette that no one paid attention to the car itself. Our exhilaration was short lived when we saw, to our horror, that Ben had caught the fishing line onto a police car. We all quickly abandoned ship, except for Ben. I dove behind an azalea bush, but I could still see through the branches that Ben was nobly trying to save King Anaboa rather than himself. He desperately held onto the line. With a glimmer of hope, and a quick act of gallantry, Ben lowered the drag on the fishing rod and gave all the slack he could, but it only took a second before the line broke and we lost King Anaboa forever. That is, until we saw the police car turn around and pull into our driveway. At that point we were all pretty well content to say we didn't want him back, or more specifically, "We've never seen that thing before in our lives!"

I'm not exactly sure what Mom's reaction was when the police officer handed her a spray-painted, rock-filled inner tube that surprisingly looked the same size as her bicycle tire, or whether Dad ever noticed our feeble attempt to wrap a now–bird's nest of knotted, stretched fishing line back onto his reel. (I don't know because I have yet to come out of those azalea bushes since 1988.)

This event, however, did introduce me to the crazy world of the human psyche, as well as teach me a deeper, more introspective lesson. We live and die by the choices we make. In this wonderful ride of life, we better know what we are holding onto and what is holding onto us. Having the proper priorities in life helps determine what things to keep and what things to let go. When life brings a little snag, sometimes the people you thought were your friends are nowhere to be found. In the end we are each held accountable for what we have made or not made of our lives. There will be a point in our lives, and in death, when we will have to stand up and fight the battle completely alone. There will only be you, God, and the decisions you have made.

# Others

## A Million-Dollar Quarter

One of my favorite books is The Giving Tree by Shel Silverstein. It's a simple story about a young boy and his tree. The young boy as a child has a great time playing with the tree, but as he grows older, the boy needs its fruit for money, its branches for a home, and its trunk for a boat. Finally, the boy is so old he only needs a place to rest, so the tree offers her stump to rest on. The Giving Tree is a great book to teach children about love and sacrificial giving.

Somewhere along the line my parents instilled in all their children the act of giving. Whether it was through examples or words, they taught us the importance of sacrificial giving. Oddly enough though, one of the best lessons I learned about giving was not from Mom and Dad, but from my little sister Elizabeth.

We were on vacation in St. Augustine, Florida. Elizabeth was four, Sam was seven, and I was probably nine years old. In order to really appreciate

44

this story, you have to understand that Elizabeth was at the age where a nickel was worth more than a dime because the nickel is bigger, and a quarter (especially in my family) was worth about a million dollars.

We woke up early one morning to tour a historical site. There was a light fog in the air as the side-street stores were opening. Dad and Sam were walking up front, I was in the middle, Mom was behind me, and Elizabeth trailed about ten feet behind Mom. Up ahead of us a store owner had just opened up and was leaning against his doorframe, enjoying the fresh morning air with a cup of coffee lazily held in his hand. When dad walked by the man he nodded a hello and in due course Sam and I did the same. It was a couple of steps after that when I heard a slight kerplunk. I looked over my shoulder to notice the man starring strangely at Elizabeth and then into his coffee. My sister in her innocence mistook the store owner for a homeless man, holding out his cup, begging for money. When she saw what she perceived as a man in need, she pulled out her million-dollar quarter and dropped it into the man's cup of coffee. We walked away as the man shook his head in bewilderment at what just happened.

If I hadn't turned around, no one would have known what Elizabeth had done because she never told anyone. She did what she thought needed to be done. Although she was young and used only a quarter, Elizabeth maturely demonstrated a valuable lesson of giving secretly, with love and sacrifice, even if it is our million-dollar quarter.

## Servant Leadership

The acronym FOCUS and its order remains true: First Things First then building relationships by serving or doing something good for Others. It is your responsibility to establish your goals in life. It is you who must take action to make things happen. It is you who must persevere through the hard times to accomplish your dreams. However, there is nothing you can accomplish without the direct involvement of others. Do you want to be rich? Then do something good for another person. Rich people simply

> "You can change you and your environment by doing this simple exercise. For the next 30 days, treat every person you meet, without exception, as the most important person on earth. You will find that people will begin treating you the same way. You see, every person IS the most important person on earth."
> Earl Nightingale

do more good for other people. Find a need and fill it. Whether you're building relationships or selling a gadget, if you find what people need or want, there is no limit to its success. The essence of any successful business, organization, or family is a serving relationship with others.

Years ago, I heard Zig Ziggler say, "If you help others get what they want in life, you can have anything and everything you want out of your life." Honestly, it made no sense to me at the time. Why should I give away something which has taken me years of study or trial and error to obtain? Why should I help other people accomplish their goals? I have my own goals! Why should I tell people how I succeeded in an area? Let them figure it out! I'm just helping my future competition. I learned the hard way, so they can too! I can tell you with complete and absolute authority that nothing is more counterproductive than that philosophy. I've discovered when I do good for other people by helping them get what they want, they return the value of my service tenfold.

> If you are interesting, people will like you, if you are interested, people will love you.

Servant leadership applies across the board in all occupations and relationships. Whether you are in education, sales, administration, management, the clergy or are building a family, find out what people need and help them get it. There is no greater asset in helping to achieve a productive and balanced life than by loving, serving, and doing good for others. Even if you say you are not a "people person," you still have to be people centered.

The Golden Rule says, "Do unto others as you would have them do unto you," but you must do it first! If you want to be first in life, put yourself last. If you want to be the greatest, be a servant to all. If you want to receive, give. If you want to get even with people, and I mean if you really want to get back at people . . . kill them with kindness, then release the hook they have in your life by forgiving them. If you want people to be kind to you, then be kind to them first! If you want people to smile at you, then smile at them first. If you want to have friends, then be a friend to someone else. People do not care how much you know until they know how much you care . . . about them!

One of the greatest cures for depression is to serve others. I wish I could better articulate the joy we receive when we focus on the needs of others. If you want to lift your spirits and experience a truly unexplainable joy, volunteer in a food shelter, help a senior citizen with yard work, read books to children, pay for the person behind you in the drive-thru line, or find a family in a restaurant and secretly pay their bill. The more you give away, the greater your capacity to give.

# "EM TUOBA TON S'TI"

One of the products we have for sale at StoriesThatTell.com is a T-shirt that reads "Em Tuoba Ton S'ti." When you stand in front of a mirror, the reflected message reads "it'S noT abouT mE." No, it's not about you. Lead by serving others.

We improve our circle of influence by serving others. You want to change the entire atmosphere of the people around you? Out-serve each other. Yes, try to out-serve your boss, co-worker, spouse, children, and friends. In doing so, you will lead by example! People don't want to be managed, they want to be led.

If you lay a rope on the floor and try to push it, only the part you're touching will move forward. But if you pull the rope, the entire length will follow you wherever your heart desires. Remember, you can never lead someone to a place you have not gone yourself. You are contagious! Light yourself on fire and people will come miles around to watch you burn. Like moths to a flame, people are attracted to winners with enthusiasm, encouragement, and excitement. Likewise, attract others to you

> "How wonderful it is that nobody need wait a single moment before starting to improve the world."
> — Anne Frank

as you lead by serving others!

## Leaders Lead with 5 H's:

For those who are visual learners, here is a five-point reference on successful leadership.

Head: Lead with vision, values, empathy, and unity. Great leaders lead with passion, encouragement, and motivation. They cast the vision where they want to go using organizational and personal values that guide their decisions. A leader leads with empathy, an attitude of understanding the other person's point of view. A leader creates an environment in which the team can unite and rally around a common cause or goal. When unity is formed, individuality is released—one can be real and true to himself if mutually assured construction is established. A unified trusting team creates open and creative individuals.

Heart: The heart of a servant; servant leadership. When one puts the needs of others first, the reward, satisfaction, and returns on that "investment" is exponentially compounded. The Law of Reciprocity is enacted when what you give comes back in return. This law, which applies in every culture on the face of the earth, simply explains that when you give something, the recipient feels an obligation to give back. The principle is that others will reciprocate in kind based on the way you treat them. This concept is exemplified in the Tale of the Eloquent Peasant, an ancient Egyptian tale, which states: "Do for one who may do for you, that you may cause him thus to do." This expectation of receiving something in return is rarely discussed openly, but nonetheless, it exists and affects negotiations and relationships.

HANDS: Practice what you preach. Great leaders actively lead by example. They pull people where they need to go rather than push them. They know that they can never take anyone further than they have gone themselves. Leaders should never be afraid to roll up their sleeves and get their hands dirty; to reach the heart of the common man, we must be capable of doing his work.

HEALTH: Personal health absolutely influences professional performance. Fill your mind, body, and spirit with the clean, the pure, the powerful, and the positive. Recognize that what goes in is what comes out. The greater the individuals' level of fitness, the greater their mental, emotional, and physical performance. As mental, emotional, and physical performance improves, so, too, does the efficiency of critical thinking and physical output, because a physically fit leader is better equipped to handle the rigorous demands placed upon him or her.

Habit: Form positive habits. Good character is formed over time through wise choices, discipline, and personal responsibility. A good leader leads through their habits. A leader knows that thoughts control actions, and actions determine character. Furthermore, those actions, good or bad, form habits that determine the course of our lives.

# Be Intentional Principle

He was the meanest kid I ever worked with. By the end of the first day, I wanted him gone. No way both of us would survive six days of camp. He was intentionally mean to other campers, he was a destructive disturbance, and he had to go back home, now!

Throughout college, I worked for the Clemson University Outdoor Laboratory, a camp and conference center. During the summer months it supported a number of "special-population" camps that focused on children with cancer, visual impairments, muscular dystrophy, and mental handicaps. Camp Sertoma, where I was working that summer, was designed for children who are either underprivileged or have a speech or hearing impairment. Sertoma campers were great kids, but a vast majority grew up in tough environments. With most campers, you could crack their hard outer shell within a few hours and consequently have a joyful and memorable week. Matthew, on the other hand, was not like any camper I had ever had. Within an hour of his arrival he had intentionally started four fights, intentionally broke toys, and seemed to intentionally tick me off. I wanted him sent back home, which was rarely done at camp. But we rarely had campers this mean!

Three days into camp, our cabin of ten-year-old boys was in total chaos due entirely to Matthew. To make matters worse, we were scheduled to camp out that night. No one wanted to be around him, much less be stuck in the woods with him. When we arrived at our campsite, we set up our shelter, made dinner over the fire, and, once it was dark, we counselors told a few stories to encourage the kids. We then rolled out our sleeping bags and called it a day. Everyone was ready for a nice, quiet sleep under the stars, but apparently Matthew had a bit more meanness he wanted to dish out.

While everyone was finding their places on the ground and settling into their sleeping bags, Matthew would walk up and kick another camper. If he didn't kick them, he would punch them in the chest or head. (Oddly enough, that was the norm for the week.) It was what he did immediately afterward that was strange: with a sincere and tender voice, he would ask his victim, "Hey, can I sleep beside you?" Of course, no one wanted him anywhere near them! In the darkness all you could hear was, "Ouch!" . . . "Can I sleep beside you?" . . . "NO!" . . . (Whack!) . . . "Can I sleep beside you?" . . . "GET AWAY!" We were all so exhausted that I had to make this madness end, so I said, "Okay . . . come HERE, Matthew. Lay down beside me!" In the blink of an eye he was next to me in his sleeping bag, and silent.

For the first time in days, everything was at peace. It was just after midnight when Matthew, the meanest kid I had ever known, taught me a lesson I have never forgotten. Everything and everyone was quiet and I was just falling asleep when I heard Matthew unzip his sleeping bag and slowly extend his hand in my direction. At that moment, I truly thought he must have smuggled a knife out of the cafeteria and was now about to stab me in the heart. However, all he did was bring out his little hand and gently place it on my chest. I lay there wide awake, my heart racing, waiting to defend a deathblow. But he kept his arm there for only a few seconds and then returned it to his sleeping bag.

I lay there for several minutes trying to process what had happened. Once again, he stretched out his arm and placed it on my chest. This time he moved his hand up to my face and touched each side. As quickly as it happened, he withdrew his hand. I lay there stunned and confused. Why was he doing this?

He performed the same little ritual several times over the course of an hour, until finally I had had enough. In a voice more annoyed than concerned, I asked, "Matthew, what are you doing? Why do you keep touching me?" What I thought he was going to do with a knife he did instead with his words, and pierced my heart. In just above a whisper, this mean little kid whom I wanted to send back home simply said, "I wanted to make sure you were still there. Every time I fell asleep, I had a nightmare that I was home. So I woke up and touched you, to make sure you were real." Tears began to pour down my face. I thought, how bad is life when home is a nightmare?

The next morning, we broke camp and headed back to our cabin. While our cabin's kids learned about archery and nature, I absorbed Matthew's case history. I had never read of such abuse and neglect. Matthew had been physically and sexually abused. He had been taken out of his home to foster care, then to a delinquency center, and then back to the home where the abuse all started. For ten years people had intentionally hurt Matthew. In turn, the only love language he knew was a punch in the face and intentional neglect. Matthew was simply replaying the messages that were recorded into him.

From that point forward, I, too, would be intentional with Matthew, only I would intentionally love, praise, listen, encourage, teach, and spend time with him. The "Be Intentional" principle then rolled over to life outside of camp. I learned to be intentional with my friends and family, coworkers and customers. I would not wait for other people to fix the problems—I would find a need and fill it. I learned to lead by example.

If you want to be the greatest in the world, serve others! If you want to be first, put yourself last! If you want to get even with those who harm you, forgive them. I decided to live intentionally. Rather than have life just happen, I decided to be proactive, not reactive.

I cannot lie and say everything was a bed of roses the rest of that week of camp, but things were considerably better. Matthew's hard shell began to fall apart, and an amazing young man began to emerge. My time

> "There are only two types of leaders: Those who believe in themselves and lift others up and those with a poor self-image who pull everybody down."
> Lou Holtz

with Matthew ended years ago, but I still find those same needs in others today. I see issues that need to be addressed and problems that need to be resolved.

I have decided to be intentional and that has made all the difference. I know this principle works, because by the end of the week, the one kid who originally fought to leave, cried to stay.

# Character

## Can I Borrow Your Space Suit?

When I was a teenager, my dad directed a team of HAZMAT specialists that control and contain hazardous and toxic spills. He had all kinds of neat safety equipment like foam, ropes, respirators, and suits. Due to safety regulations, Dad would often have to retire old or used equipment. It was one of those retirement occasions that I borrowed one of what I called his "space suits." The suit was perfect! It was light blue with a large hump on the back for an air tank, shoes and gloves attached to the body, and a head with a large plastic face shield for easy viewing. Anyone who put it on looked like the robot in the old TV series Lost in Space. In order to wear it—and live—you had to have some sort of breathing apparatus, because once you were zipped in, it was airtight. When I first got the suit, I wasn't fully aware of this minor yet significant detail, but I can now confirm this with full authority and experience. (Children, do not try this at home.)

Later on, when I was in college, I tanned animal hides to use as a teaching tool for children. I didn't want to kill the animals, so I used my most bountiful resource, Interstate 85 and Highway 123 in Clemson, South Carolina. The highways and back roads were my canvas, and fresh roadkill was my palette. I collected just about every known animal that was stupid enough to walk in front of a car: beavers, woodchucks, deer, opossum, foxes, and rabbits. If you could kill it at 60 miles an hour without it exploding, I got it. Unfortunately, I didn't have a skunk in my repertoire. So when the door of opportunity opened, I pulled over.

It was a beautiful sunny afternoon as I was traveling down I-85 to York Place Children's Home when I discovered my first skunk roadkill. Being the "always-on-the-lookout-for-roadkill" kind of guy, I was prepared with three large plastic bags. I discovered the freshly killed skunk on the edge of the road and quickly pulled over to wrap my treasure in the bags. It's actually a skillful art, to not draw attention to yourself as you pick up a dead skunk off the side of a major interstate. Proud of myself, I tossed my prize in the backseat of the rental car and continued down the road. It was precisely 4.3 miles before I became respectfully amazed at the absolute potency of a dead skunk in a confined space. My drive from Clemson to York took about two hours. The skunk enjoyed about six minutes of it.

Not only was I frustrated and angry with myself that I had to toss out my prize at 75 miles an hour, but I had also ruined the fresh "like-new" smell of the rental car. "It was horrible! I almost died!" I told the rental store. "I've read there was a rabid skunk in the area. Just my luck to have a crazy skunk jump in my backseat." I guess I should consider it a blessing I made it out alive.

The smell that permeated out of my skin for days only strengthened my resolve to find another skunk. I vowed next time to be prepared. In a stroke of pure genius, I remembered my dad's space suit. Being the intellectual college student, I logically deduced, if nothing can go out, then nothing can come in . . . thus making the space suit the perfect skunk suit! I excitedly drove to Spartanburg that weekend, grabbed my dad's suit, drove back to Clemson, and awaited the scent.

It wasn't long before the intoxicating aroma of a freshly killed skunk was in the air. I found my long-awaited prize, and, now wise to plastic bags, tossed the carcass in the back of Ole Bessie, my prize-winning-roadkill pickup truck. I pulled up behind my apartment at the pig farm and found a cozy little place in the woods. I had already anticipated all the complexities and scenarios of skinning a skunk, but I had not entertained the thought of explaining to someone why I was hiding in the woods, on a pig farm, wearing an E.T.-looking space suit, while skinning a skunk. I doubted anyone would find me, but I thought the camouflage face paint wouldn't hurt.

Between my held breaths of air, I quickly prepared the final touches of my makeshift skinning table. Once all was in place, I rushed inside to the smell-safe haven of my room. I zipped myself securely in the suit, making sure all openings were totally closed to prevent the smell from coming in and interrupting the processes. I then waddled my way to the skinning table and began the procedure.

Finally, after all this time, I was about to have a skunk in my repertoire. Life was good and I cherished the moment. I felt pretty good knowing that as I stood there in the space suit breathing my fresh air, there, just millimeters away was a smell that could gag a sewer rat.

Everything started off fine, but the suit was beginning to get a little hot. About five minutes into the procedure, flies and bees were everywhere, and condensation began to form on the inside of the face shield. Ten minutes passed and I began to get lightheaded. I thought it was odd that I was having a very difficult time concentrating on what I was doing. I tried to work faster, but it was hard to see through the water droplets that now totally covered the shield. The only way I could see through it was by pressing my face against it and using my nose as a human windshield wiper. I felt very sleepy, but at the same time, I couldn't stop laughing at the hissing and wheezing sounds my breath made as I tried to inhale. I had the oddest sensation that I couldn't breathe.

I'm not sure where the voice came from. I don't know if it was God—maybe it came when I started answering questions the skunk was asking me, or maybe it was the rock I hit when I lost consciousness—but all I know is that I heard a still small voice say, "Uhhh, uhhh, Thomas? Just want you to know, you're, uhhh, suffocating." In my half-comatose state, I was able to get up off the ground, stumble to my feet and reach the zipper by my head. In a desperate act of survival I quickly yanked the zipper down. I turned my face toward the opening and with all my might, I sucked in what I thought would be a rush of sweet spring breeze. For one glorious tenth of a second, it was the richest, freshest air my lungs have ever enjoyed. And then it hit me like a Mack truck. The liquefied putrid skunk smell began to flood into my gasping lungs. The potency of the odor was so strong it burnt my eyes like a cut onion, my nose like a whiff of ammonia, and my throat like a shot of Rock and Rye. Then everything went black.

~

When I came to, I found that my body had fallen on top of the skinning table and my face had landed neatly on top of the skunk. I felt skunk, I saw skunk, I smelled skunk, and I tasted skunk. I do not like skunks; as a matter of fact, I nearly vomit now when I do smell one. In the end I just wrapped everything up and put it in the freezer. There it remains to this very day.

~

It is that still small voice that we choose to listen to or not in times of decision. Your character is created and shaped by what you've done or haven't done when you think no one is watching. We must choose to do right with the little or "hidden" things in life so as to prepare ourselves for the large and public decisions.

A leader's focus is grounded on a foundation of character and moral integrity. If you have integrity, nothing else matters. If you don't have integrity, nothing else matters. The more integrity you have, the less paperwork you need. Character is not formed in times of adversity, but it is revealed. In fact, Abraham Lincoln once wrote, "Nearly all men can stand adversity, but if you want to test a man's character, give him power."

If you hold a full glass of water and you get bumped, what comes out? The water, of course! Likewise, what's inside of you is what comes out when you get "bumped." For example, if you always tell the truth, you never have to remember what you've said. Without a well-grounded character, life gets out of balance, and it doesn't take long for things to fall apart. Remember, character is a lot easier kept than it is retrieved. Jim Rohn, an American entrepreneur, author, and speaker, states it well: "Character isn't something you were born with and can't change. It's something you weren't born with and must take responsibility for forming."

In the end, our thoughts control our decisions, our decisions control our character, and our character controls our actions. Ultimately, our life is defined by the actions we take or do not take. People want to be led, not managed, and you lead them first with your character.

> Having a strong work ethic is a MUST. "Genius is 1% inspiration and 99% perspiration."
> Henry Ford

Many companies try to find customers first and then hope to build a relationship. A more viable way of business, however, is building a relationship first then hoping they become a customer. Any lasting relationship is built on service and character. If you are selling a product, people will always remember the quality and service long after they forget the price. If you can provide a high-quality product with great service built on indelible character, there is no limit to its success.

Three traits must be fostered for a successful

personal or team relationship.

1. The relationship is built on the assurance that each party will give 100 percent effort and is committed to excellence.

2. Great emphasis is placed on serving and encouraging each other to higher levels of productivity (mutually assured construction).

3. Each person knows they can fully trust the other.

# Termite Races

I am fascinated by the similarities between animal and human communication. I've especially noticed this similarity with horses. My first experience with horses was riding one upside down in an international bareback rodeo competition; consequently, I have great admiration for the animal. A fascinating quality about these animals holds true to human interaction as well. Like all humans, every horse looks for two things, security and leadership. To break a horse, or as Monty Roberts, author of The Man Who Listens to Horses, calls it, "joining up," you must first show the horse that you will protect it and that it is secure in your presence. Second, you must show it that you can, and will, lead it. Those same characteristics are what human beings seek as well:

am I secure in your presence, and will you lead me to greener pastures? Napoleon Bonaparte said basically the same thing: "Men are moved by two levers only: fear and self-interest."

Even insects display the same desire for security and leadership. Have you ever raced termites? Termites and many other insects secrete a pheromone, leaving an invisible "trail" for others to follow. (You'll also notice this phenomenon with a line of ants.) Next time you're out in the woods, grab a few termites under a rotting log. Put them in a container, then find yourself a sheet of paper and a "Bic" ink pin. It just so happens that the chemicals in a Bic pen are similar enough to termites' pheromone that you can trick them to follow you wherever you lead it. (A few other brands will work as well, but you'll have to experiment.)

Place a termite on the sheet of paper, being gentle not to crush the little fella. Then let it walk around a minute or two. At this point the termite has no direction to follow. It is desperately searching for the security of its colony and the leadership to get there. Now start a line of ink just in front of the predicted path of the termite. It may take a few tries, but the termite will soon follow the ink line wherever you draw it. If you draw a circle, the termite will just keep going around and around. If you want to get creative, get a few friends together and have a termite race!

Just like termites, people are desperately searching for leadership, leadership they can follow because of the character you have established.

Years ago, I had the pleasure of working with the Chick-fil-A corporation. I found that founder Truett Cathy and his multibillion-dollar company hire based on three C's: Character, Competency, and Compatibility. Cathy stated, "People need to be competent in their education and can be trained to do the work. They of course need to be compatible with the team. But one thing we can't teach is character. Either they have it or they don't."

A dear friend of mine discovered that principle when he found that an employee had embezzled tens of thousands of dollars from his

> "How few there are who have courage enough to own their own faults, or resolution enough to mend them."
> Ben Franklin

company. The employee was more than competent and was very compatible with the other staff, but his lack of character eroded all those attributes. Unfortunately, as I write this, it has been discovered that a staff member of an organization I was once part of embezzled more than $500,000. There is no way to determine the full amount of damage she has done to the organization, her family, or the "friends" who trusted her. Character truly does count!

# Communication

## April's Fool

He went out of his way to embarrass me and make me the butt of a joke. If I walked by him he would trip me with his cane. If I mingled past him he would wrap his arms around my head and give me a noogie headlock. He was a mean old cuss, but I loved him for it. Rex was small but had the heart of a bull-dog. His wit was fast as a viper, and to smooth things over he displayed the smile of a gentleman. His body indicated he was in his eighties, but his joyful and mischievous spirit fooled everyone into thinking he was still a teenager.

Rex and I cut up all the time. I actually looked forward to his shenanigans each week. I promised him I would get him back one day. "Mean old man, picking on a poor little kid like me," I would say. "Just you wait . . . when you're not around all your near-to-death friends, I'll get you!" Rex would just smile, and out of the side of his mouth, he would challenge, "Bring it on, whipper-snapper!" That's how most of our conversations ended each week, and I wouldn't expect to see or hear from Rex until the next Sunday. However, on a beautiful Saturday afternoon in April, our paths would cross and I would finally have the chance to take the upper hand.

I was digging in my garden when I looked up and saw ole Rex walking down my avenue. What a surprise! I had never seen him walking in my neighborhood before, but it was great to see him walking about. He wore his trademark plaid golf cabbie hat, pulled down near his failing eyes. There in his right hand, supporting every other step, was his infamous snaring cane.

The sight of his cane brought back embarrassing memories of trips, yanks, and jerks. In the safety of my garden, it also gave me a flood of devious ideas for retribution. Because Rex's eyes were not that great, I knew if I disguised my voice, I could take advantage of the opportunity to give my dear old friend a well-deserved hard time.

I grabbed my shovel, bowed up my chest, and with a loud, demanding, authoritative voice I hollered, "HEY, OLD MAN! DON'T YOU KNOW YOUR KIND IS NOT ALLOWED IN THIS NEIGHBORHOOD?" My poor old friend stopped in his tracks. I was proud that I had not broken into laughter. He turned toward me and with a crack in his voice, he asked, "Are you talking to me?" I had him right where I wanted him. I figured he would get me back later, but I would enjoy this as long as I could. I snapped back at him, "YEAH, I'm talking to YOU! WE DON'T WANT YOU AROUND HERE! YOU'RE NOT SUPPOSED TO BE WALKING MY STREET! GET ON OUT OF HERE!" I continued toward him, bowing up a little more and walking faster. "YOU HEARD ME! GET!" He began to stutter a bit and looked around confused: "Wha . . . What do you mean? I . . . I just . . . Can't I . . . Please don't . . ." Boy, did I have him going!

As I swung my shovel around, I could tell my friend had just about reached his cardiac limit. On the inside I could hardly contain myself! This was, by far, the best joke I had ever pulled . . . but I was surprised he had not recognized me yet! I chimed a few more words like, "Keep on walking! Who do you THINK you are?" I marched closer toward him, and as I neared about ten feet, I raised the shovel over my head as if to whack him with it. My intent was to scare him with a pretend deathblow, then drop the shovel and give him a big hug. I figured the closer I got to him, the more likely he would be to recognize me—and the funnier the joke would become.

I kind of felt sorry for little old Rex. His poor arms were shaking as he lifted his cane in defense. I'm sure he thought I was some psycho about to hack him. Man, were we going to have a good laugh with this one!

In what must have been to him his last battle in a crazy world, Rex raised his arms, straightened his back, and lifted his head. The old golfer's hat that once shielded the face of my old friend now revealed the face of a man terrified for his life. To my horror, it also revealed the face of a man that was not my friend, but of a man I had never met before . . . a perfect stranger! All he wanted was a nice quiet walk in the neighborhood. All I wanted was a rock to crawl under.

Like my friend Rex, things are rarely what they seem to be. Oftentimes we think we have everything figured out. Unfortunately, most live life only to discover that things didn't turn out quite like they had planned. In regard to leadership, clarity is a rarity, and the lack of communication is the leading cause of that malady. Ninety-nine percent of all problems can be boiled down to a communication problem. If things did not turn out the way you had planned, first reevaluate how you communicated and try to understand the recipient's perspective. Clear communication is essential to success. Research carried out by the Carnegie Institute of Technology, for example, shows that only 15 percent of your financial success will be due to your technical skills, while 85 percent will originate from your people skills—communication, attitude, enthusiasm, and self-discipline.

All of us in our narcissistic nature believe that once we have given instructions, everyone completely understands, agrees, and is even capable of reading our minds for the unspoken requests. We often assume people understand what we are thinking, because if we think, feel, or value it, other people will of course do the same. As you will see in our discussion of personality types, 75 percent of what you say, feel, and expect of people is not completely understood the way you intended

Ask any real-estate broker and they will tell you a good real-estate investment first starts with three essential elements: Location, Location, Location. Three essential elements are required in any successful relationship as well: Communication, Communication, Communication. Remember, the core of any successful business, organization, church, or family rests predominantly on successful relationships. Everything rises and falls with leadership, leadership rises and falls with relationships, and relationships rise and fall with communication.

The communication principle is perfectly displayed in the Biblical account of the Tower of Babel. Genesis 11 gives an account of the whole world having one language, a common speech. It then explains that the people set to build a tower to heaven and make a name for themselves. God saw what they were doing and said, "If as one people speaking the same language they have begun to do this, then nothing they plan to do will be impossible for them" (Genesis 11:6, NIV). The people's languages were then changed and the tower was never completed, but the principle remains—nothing is possible when communication is unclear. And nothing is impossible when people have a common goal with clear communication. Remember, a unified and trusting team creates open and creative individuals.

# PERSONALITY STYLES

It is paramount that you take the time to understand personality traits and their connection to clear communication. Remember . . . clarity is a rarity! You may have sent a message, but the crucial question is, was it received? When you understand personality traits, you:

1. Become a better communicator. It's difficult to communicate effectively with people you don't understand, and it's easy to misinterpret someone whose personality is the opposite of yours. Once you understand how personality styles work, you can adapt your own style to unlock better communication. You will understand to speak more directly or indirectly. You can assign jobs that are more task or people oriented.

2. Can resolve or prevent conflicts. When you understand why someone did or said something due to a personality trait, you will be less likely to react negatively. An awareness of another's underlying motivations can allow you to diffuse problems before they start.

3. Gain credibility and positively influence others. Every interaction you have with others either increases or decreases your credibility and influence. By knowing another's personality style, you can immediately gain credibility and influence by adapting to his or her style.

# Personality Types

You can spend a lifetime studying personality types and take a number of tests to determine your style. The subject is far too comprehensive to go into extensive detail within this book. However, if you have never studied this amazing subject matter, let me whet your pallet with an overview.

DISC is a group of psychological inventories developed in 1958 by John Geier, Ph.D., who based his research off the work of psychologist William Moulton Marston. The DISC assessment divides personality styles into four basic categories: Outgoing, Reserved, Task-Oriented, and People-Oriented. All individuals possess all four, but what differs from one person to another is the extent of each. According to Geier's research, most people have a distinct or primary type followed by a lesser type or a mixture of two. Keep in mind, each of our personalities or the way in which we respond or react to a situation is a blend of types and will vary depending on the environment we are in.

For more than ten years, I have studied hundreds of resources, attended education classes, and have led countless seminars on personality types and how they relate to leadership. The following brief synopsis of the four personality types is a compilation of information from my personal experience as well as research from a number of resources (Geier Learning International, Inscape Publishing, and Personality Insights Inc.). You can also search the web for "DISC" and "personality types" to find thousands of resources and tests to develop your understanding of this valuable leadership tool.

An outgoing type of person would be the first to take charge, speak up in the group, crack a joke, or introduce themselves, while an individual with a more reserved personality will wait and get the feel of the group before speaking up, if at all. Those with a reserved trait prefer working by themselves, in small groups, or behind the scenes.

A task-oriented personality is a direct communicator and is focused on order and consisten-cy- a work-first-play-later mentality. People-oriented personalities are indirect communicators and are fo-cused more on having fun, building relationships and cooperation, over completing a task.

## 4 Basic Personality Types

| Outgoing/ Task Oriented | Outgoing/ People Oriented |
|---|---|
| Bold Direct Dominant Demanding Competitive Being in Charge *Needs: Results* *Battleship* | Expressive Friendly Outgoing Emotional Approval Influence *Needs: People* *Cruise Ship* |
| **Reserved/ Task Oriented** | **Reserved/ People Oriented** |
| Technical Cautious Logical Consistent Excellence Detailed *Needs: Quality* *Submarine* | Supportive Steady Team player Service Sincere Loyal *Needs: Cooperation* *Sailboat* |

The following charts help put the four dimensions of personality into perspective:

# The Dominant (D)-Battleship Type:

| | |
|---|---|
| Words to Describe Their Leadership: | Dominant, Direct, Demanding, Decisive, Determined, Doer, Bold, Forceful, Strong-willed |
| Their Mindset: | Get it done! Make it happen! Play to win! Results! |
| Their Likes: | Activities, Competition, Hard work, Doing things, Challenges, Getting results, Being in charge, Accomplishing tasks, Administration |
| Their Dislikes | Inefficiency, Indecision |
| They Are: | Goal-oriented, Hard to please, Self-confident, Firm, Industrious, Performance conscious, Determined |
| Out of Control: | Dictator |
| Motivated by: | Conquering challenges, Choices, Control, Solving problems |
| Environmental Needs: | Freedom, Authority, Varied activities, Opportunities for advancement |

| Primary Needs and Expectations of Others: | Results |
|---|---|
| Communication Style: | Straightforward communication |
| Fears: | Being disrespected or not winning |
| Need to Learn to: | Be sensitive to people, Be able to relax, Be patient, Speak "softer," Let other people share control |
| Challenges: | Impatient, Insensitive, Poor listener |

# The Inspiring (I) - Cruise Ship Type:

| | |
|---|---|
| Words to Describe Their Leadership: | Inspiring, Influencing, Important, Interactive, Impressive, Interested in people, Spontaneous, Optimistic, Talkative, Expressive, Friendly, Outgoing, Emotional, Persuading, Enthusiasm, Entertaining |
| Their Mindset: | To be the star of the show . . . fun and excitement! |
| Their Likes: | Exposure to people, Short-term projects, Making people laugh, Doing things, Lots of activities, To be on the go, Talking with people, Prestige, To be important, To have fun, To be liked, To create excitement |
| Their Dislikes | Routines, Complexity |
| They Are: | Talkative, Great starters, Likeable, Prone to exaggerate, Easily excitable, Fun to watch |
| Out of Control: | Unfocused |
| Motivated by: | Recognition, Approval, Popularity, Fun |

| Environmental Needs: | Prestige, Friendly relationships, Opportunities to influence others, Opportunities to inspire others, Chances to verbalize ideas |
|---|---|
| Primary Needs and Expectations of Others: | People and Flexible |
| Communication Style: | Friendly and informal |
| Fears: | Being disliked or confined by rules |
| Need to Learn to: | Better manage time, Be more realistic, Listen to others, Stay focused and complete tasks |
| Challenges: | Lack of detail, Short attention span, Low follow-through |

# The Supportive (S) - Sailboat Type:

| | |
|---|---|
| Words to Describe Their Leadership: | Supportive, Steady, Stable, Sweet, Sensitive, Sentimental, Conferring, Sincere, Loyal, Practical, Good listener, Patient, Team player, Service, Diplomatic |
| Their Mindset: | Neutral, Let's all get along with each other!, No conflict |
| Their Likes: | Peace, An even pace, Harmony, Reassurance, Friendly groups, Teamwork, Helping others, Cooperation, Minimize confrontation |
| Their Dislikes: | Insensitivity, Impatience |
| They Are: | Team-oriented, Friendly, Cooperative, Loyal friends, Sensitive to others' needs, Understanding, Accepting, Helpful to others, Peace maintaining |
| Out of Control: | Indecision |
| Motivated by: | Security, Appreciation, Assurance, Acceptance |

| | |
|---|---|
| Environmental Needs: | An area of specialization, Identification with a group, Established work pattern, Stability of situation, Consistent environment |
| Primary Needs and Expectations of Others: | Cooperation |
| Communication Style: | Warm, Open, Sincere communication |
| Fears: | Confrontation and change |
| Need to Learn to: | Deal with change, Be able to say "No!," Decide and act independently, Hold other people accountable for their actions |
| Challenges: | Oversensitive, Slow to begin, Dislikes change |

# The Cautious (C) - Submarine Type:

| | |
|---|---|
| Words to Describe Their Leadership: | Cautious, Calculating, Competent, Consistent, Contemplative, Careful, Methodical, Technical, Logical, Precise, Sensitive, and Analytical |
| Their Mindset: | Let's do things right and with excellence. What is the plan? Have you thought things through? What is the purpose behind this? Why? |
| Their Likes: | Consistency, Excellent work, Being accurate, Information/Data, Value, Quality, Getting things right, Having a plan, Procedure, Honesty |
| Their Dislikes | Disorganization, Impropriety |
| They Are: | Procedure-oriented, Dedicated to the task, Focused on the details, Logical, Accurate, Respectful, Systems and planning oriented |
| Out of Control: | Too critical |
| Motivated by: | Quality answers, Excellence, Value, Accuracy |

| | |
|---|---|
| Environmental Needs: | Clearly defined tasks, Sufficient time and resources to accomplish tasks, Freedom to ask questions, Limited risks, Assignments that require planning and precision |
| Primary Needs and Expectations of Others: | Following procedure and quality |
| Communication Style: | Logical, Precise, and Detailed |
| Fears: | Being inconsistent/wrong or illogical |
| Need to Learn to: | Not over-analyze, Not be a perfectionist, Express feelings, Trust others, Be more flexible, Lighten up and have more fun |
| Challenges: | Perfectionism, Critical, Unresponsive |

# Birds Of A Feather

One summer my family and I were visiting the beautiful white beaches of Naples, Florida. We found a secluded strip of beach that had the Gulf on one side and a little lagoon on the other. It was the ideal spot for our children to play in the Gulf, my wife to enjoy her book, and me to watch the wildlife in the lagoon. I am constantly amazed at the lessons we can learn if we simply sit still, close our mouths, listen, and watch. I've never learned anything while talking.

Shortly after we settled in and things calmed down from any disruption we may have caused, I was able to enjoy the life that called the lagoon home. Suddenly, out of nowhere, a loon popped to the surface of the water. The slick, half-submerged, swimming water bird came up briefly and then just as quickly, submerged and came up again a hundred feet away with a small fish. Just beyond the loon, my eye caught sight of a posing crane on the edge of the bank. Like the hands on a clock, he moved methodically and slowly. In a blink of an eye, his long beak pierced the water and he quickly swallowed a tiny fish. My fascination with the crane was interrupted when a kingfisher broke my viewing plane. It was a cocky looking bird. He zipped from one side of the lagoon to the other, where he dove off the tree branches and just grazed the top of the water to catch his prey. What a beautiful sight, to see three different birds using their unique skills to survive in the lagoon. I was smiling at the revelation when a shadow passed over me, into the lagoon and disappearing into the trees. An osprey with its enormous wingspan was cruising the surrounding area for a catch. I had seen this type of bird on TV but never in real life. She was majestic yet prehistoric. In an instant, she dove from the sky toward the lagoon. The fish she plucked from the water appeared almost too heavy for her to fly with, but she quickly regained her strength and flew out of sight.

People's personalities and methods of communication are very similar to the birds in the lagoon. We all have unique styles and personalities. We have different ways of doing things and different talents we can use on the fly. A leader's focus is found in a leader who can recognize those unique differences and talents, and position people in their correct roles based on those talents. Remember, there is no such thing as a bad job—rather, it's just the wrong person doing the job. What may seem like torture to some is joy to others. What is easy and second nature to one is drudgery and causes stress to another.

# Consumption

Financial discipline and responsible consumption of goods is one of the greatest tools of a leader and one that most people overlook, deny, or place out of order. I often jokingly say that adults are nothing but teenagers with wrinkled skin. Do we ever grow out of the teenage mentality? Every day I meet teenagers walking around in adult bodies, bodies that are mature with age but mentally have the discipline and self-control of high-schoolers. Maturity, however, is having the foresight to deny yourself what you want now so you can have far more later. Life is a balance between what you want and what you're willing to give up. The "I want it now. I deserve it. It's my right to have it!" mentality causes self-imposed slavery. We are very quick to claim our rights and privileges but slow to claim responsibility. One of the greatest tools of A Leader's FOCUS is freedom and more specifically, financial freedom!

Steve Siebold, in his book How Rich People Think, very eloquently puts it this way: "Unless you're living in poverty, making more money will not make you happier. It will, however, give you more choices. Some people enjoy big houses and shiny cars, while others could care less about material possessions. But what citizen of the world living in the 21st century wouldn't choose to be free? Free to do what you want to do, when you want to do it, for as long as you want to do it. Who would deny themselves this kind of freedom? Only one group: people who don't believe it's possible."

The Bible talks more about money and its pitfalls than it does about heaven. According to Proverbs 22:7, "The rich rules over the poor, and the borrower is slave to the lender" (NIV). If you want to have the freedom to do what you love, with the ones you love, you have to live below your means. Simply put, "act your wage!" as financial expert Dave Ramsey says. It breaks my heart when I hear people say, "I hate Sundays because I know I have to work on Monday." People are "enslaved" to their jobs because they have to make car payments they never should have had, or mortgages they could not afford. We buy things we don't need, spend money we don't have, and try to impress people we don't even like.

If you want a leader's focus, you have to acknowledge the importance of being in control of your money. Growing up, I would often hear from my sisters, "Mind your own business!" It's true, you should mind your own business . . . and your business is you. Grow up and know where your money is going and growing. If you don't know what to do, then surround yourself with wise counsel that will help teach—not tell—you what to do. Remember that getting-rich-quick schemes will get you poorer even quicker. If you are married, communicate with your spouse about your finances (for some, that means shut up and listen). I know for a fact my wife has saved us tens of thousands of dollars by listening to her intuition.

Here's a quick reality check with money and the importance of managing it.

- According to NLI Research and the USDC, the average Japanese household saves 17.9 percent of after-tax income. The average household in Europe saves 8–12 percent. The average U.S. household saves . . . -3 percent. (Yep, that's a negative 3 percent!).

- 75% of Americans live paycheck to paycheck (survey by Careerbuilder.com).

- 86% of divorces are due to financial mismanagement (The Credit and Financial Management Review).

- 64% of Americans do not have $1,000 in the bank to cover an unexpected expense (National Foundation for Credit Counseling).

The principle of living under your means and living off a budget, which the late financial advisor Larry Burkett defined as simply "telling your money what to do," makes complete sense to most everyone. But once again, what we believe in principal is not what we do in practice. I can beat over your head the financial advantages of being debt free, but unless you understand in your heart the Law of Diminishing Returns, none of it will matter. Economically speaking, this law is a classic economic concept that states: as more investment in an area is made, overall return on that investment decreases assuming that all variables remain fixed. However, I am referring to my philosophical Law of Diminishing Returns which states: All things that return pleasure diminish over time. In other words, nothing on this earth will give you pleasure forever, and our pleasure in something will always diminish. Every material thing will give satisfaction only temporarily.

Some people's definition of success is to get more so as to spend more: "If I work hard enough, long enough, get enough things, reach a certain position . . ."; "If I just had _____ then I would be happy." This worldview is not only a misconception but a lie we tell ourselves. If this definition were true, then why do we buy the newer, better things? We buy a house, car, phone, clothes, gadgets, etc. and satisfaction is filled temporarily, only to diminish until we buy something new. Let me repeat it this way: if you are trying to find "lasting happiness" in *things,* you will never find it.

Don't get me wrong, there is nothing wrong with having things as long as those things do not have you. Live below your means before you try to increase your means. Use your blessings to bless others. As I recall, I have never seen a U-Haul truck follow a hearse. When you took in your first breath, you had nothing, and as you breath out your last, you'll have the same.

The only exception I have found with this Law of Diminishing Returns is the return on relationships. A healthy and productive relationship (God, spouse, children, family, and friends) can and should increase in satisfaction over time. From the hundreds of thousands of people I have surveyed, 10 to 1 would rather have healthy relationships over money in the bank.

Napoleon Hill once said, "No more effort is required to aim high in life, to demand abundance and prosperity, than is required to accept misery and poverty." Similarly, Jessie Belle Rittenhouse correctly stated this universal truth through these lines:

I bargained with Life for a penny,
And Life would pay no more,
However I begged at evening
When I counted my scanty store.
For Life is a just employer,
He gives you what you ask,
But once you have set the wages,
Why, you must bear the task.
I worked for a menial's hire,
Only to learn, dismayed,
That any wage I had asked of Life,
Life would have willingly paid.

Money is a tool and when managed properly, it can bring great freedom. Financial freedom opens doors that are not constrained by what you have to do because of debt obligations. You are free to pursue your calling with little constraints.

# Understanding

Recanting the war tales of the Roman Empire, Dan Carlin, in his "Hardcore History" podcasts, said, "You can train, have a fancy spear and armor . . . but at the end of the day when one spear was heading for another spear . . . what really mattered was what was under the helmet."

Years ago, I had the pleasure of meeting Tony Dungy and Peyton Manning from the Indianapolis Colts. I asked Peyton, "What makes you such a successful quarterback?" He said, "Thomas, long before the defense ever moves, I know what they're going to do. I'm able to change the play on the fly because I've studied their plays. I think what makes me different is not necessarily my arm, but that I'm always seeking understanding." Even during the game, as soon as Peyton gets off the field, someone hands him pictures of what the defense is doing. He is in constant pursuit of understanding.

Stop learning, and you stop growing; stop growing and you stop living. Every living thing is in constant change. How arrogant we are to expect the world to change around us while we are unwilling to change ourselves. In reality, there are no plateaus in life. You are either going up or going down. You are either growing physically, mentally, emotionally, and spiritually, or you are atrophying. Fruit is either ripening or rotting. The one thing that will help in keeping the growth is the constant pursuit of understanding.

Always seek understanding—not so much to seek "information" but to seek understanding. The difference between information and understanding is subtle but important. It could be the difference between success and failure. You might fill your mind with information, but understanding is what you do and how you make meaning out of the information. I have known quite a few people with Ph.D.'s who work alongside others with barely a high-school education; they have the head knowledge but do not know how to apply the information. Similarly, I know people with barely a high-school education who are wildly successful running their own business or managing a company. You might know everything in this world, but if you can't apply it, you know nothing.

A leader's focus is always in pursuit of understanding. There is truly an infinite amount of knowledge to obtain and discover. The more you learn, the more connections you'll find with other material, which opens the door for more understanding. I have often compared the human mind to a lava lamp. As the light heats up, the substance in the bottom of the jar begins to heat up and form blobs, which slowly rise to the top. As other blobs rise, they combine to form even larger blobs. Like the lamp, as we learn, a blob of information is formed in our minds. As we continue to learn, connections are formed, resulting in limitless possibilities.

Authorities often maintain that short-term storage in our minds is physiologically an electrochemical process, whereas long-term storage requires protein synthesis for maintaining information over extended periods of time. The jump between information that is electrochemical and information that requires protein synthesis is made when sensory connections are formed.

While teaching algebra, algebra II, geometry, biology, and chemistry, I was excited to find the students leaving with frontal lobe headaches. The core processes of memory are encoding, storage, and retrieval, all of which occur in the frontal lobe of the brain. Similarly, it is difficult to blow up a balloon for the first time. However, each time it expands and deflates, it takes less effort. Learning new things can be difficult, but the constant pursuit of understanding and making connections is in direct correlation with our innovation, invention, efficiency, and success. With new information comes new inspiration!

Seek to know everything you can within your vocation. Knowledge is power, and the more you know, the more confident you'll become. The more you learn, the more you earn. A poor salary is the price you pay for ignorance. In the information age in which we now live, you will be paid more for what you know than what you do. To gather, analyze, apply, and assess information is a skill that truly belongs to the information age. Understanding of today demands the understanding of the day before.

The pursuit of understanding is not just confined to science or careers. Ralph Waldo Emerson once wrote, "Every man is my superior in that I can learn something from him." Lessons can constantly be learned by observing the world around you and especially the people in it. Regardless of their age or position, you can learn something from everyone! Word to the wise: The best advice you will ever receive is that advice that you seek out. Beware of advice that seeks you out. Remember, it's the empty wagon that makes the most noise.

It's also a mighty thin pancake that doesn't have two sides, so let's flip this proverbial pancake!

Warning! In times of change, your "experience" can be your worst ally. Sometimes the more you learn, the more you learn of "limits" or what you think "cannot be done." As a grad student at Clemson University, I was fortunate enough to help build an experimental machine that could grow plants in months compared to the traditional means that took years. Doctorates of Biology, Tissue Culture, Meteorology, and Engineering were organized to complete and manufacture this well-funded invention. Quite frankly, I was the lowest on the totem pole of education. It was my job to construct and test the designs. Though I had an undergrad in Horticulture, I had very little knowledge of the other fields of expertise. More specifically, I had very little knowledge of what "couldn't" be done. Thankfully, I was given the freedom to question and improve the experiments. I was told several times that my ideas wouldn't or couldn't work. Some of my ideas didn't work, but quite a few proved to be possible and in fact better than those of the current procedure. Unlike the doctorates, I did not understand what I "could not" do. I was not aware of the limitations and therefore had none.

I once had the pleasure of giving a keynote to the coaches and staff of the University of Notre Dame. While doing research for my presentation, I ran across information regarding the building process of The Word of Life mosaic, affectionately called "Touchdown Jesus." The artist Millard Sheets was commissioned for the project, a mural composed of 324 panels, of which 135 are solid granite and Mankato stone. In order to match Sheets' rendering, the granite had to be cut in curves. What's interesting is until then, the ability to cut curves in granite had been considered impossible. Engineering students who were working on Sheets' project were told to cut the granite to the desired specifications. Not aware of this "impossibility," the students designed such a machine.

∼

May 6, 1954. On that day in less than four minutes, the long-held scientific limits of the human body were shattered forever. It previously had been said that the human heart could not withstand the stress of such a feat, but on a track in Oxford, England, Roger Bannister broke the four-minute mile. It was the first in human history and was thought to have been impossible. Remarkably, 46 days later an Australian, John Landy, also broke the four-minute mile, and in less than a year after him, six others did the same.

People often forget that Roger Bannister was criticized for his "unconventional" style of training. Remember, the price you pay for stepping outside the bounds of "normal" is criticism. Bannister later became a neurologist because, as he said, "you never reach the end of learning and how to do things better. I undertook a deliberate challenge that I would never achieve. I think that's very good to be put in your place in that way."

Always seek understanding, but also recognize we truly have no clue of our possibilities. It is said our brain contains more than 100 billion neurons. Attached to each neuron are 50,000 dendrites. Each one of those dendrites can connect to any other dendrite in any combination of ways greater than the number of atoms in the universe (it is estimated there are $1 \times 10^{80}$ atoms in the observable universe). That huge number of synapses firing and connections being made are all happening in something that can be held in one hand.

$\sim$

Only five men had succeeded in swimming the English Channel. The medical consensus at the time was that only men could accomplish such a feat. Doctors had concluded that women did not possess the muscle strength or stamina to swim the distance. However, on August 6, 1926, 20-year-old Gertrude Ederle not only swam the English Channel but beat the record by more than two hours.

Ms. Ederle swam the treacherous stretch under adverse conditions, battling riptides, crosscurrents, driving rain, and heavy seas, as well as constant threat of floating debris, poisonous jellyfish, and sharks. Because of the stormy weather, she had swum 35 miles in crossing the 21-mile-wide channel. Yet her time stood for 24 years before it was broken in 1950 by Florence Chadwick. During some of the toughest moments, her trainer tried to get her to give up. "I'd just look at him and say, 'What for?'" Ederle recalled. "People said women couldn't swim the channel; I proved they could."

~

After the death of his father King David, a young Solomon was granted an invitation from God to "Ask for whatever you want me to give you." Rather than long life, wealth, or death of his enemies, Solomon asked for a discerning heart to govern and to distinguish between right and wrong. Allow me to close this section on understanding by once again quoting from the wisest man to have ever lived.

Listen, my sons, to a father's instruction;
> pay attention and gain understanding.

I give you sound learning,
> so do not forsake my teaching.

When I was a boy in my father's house, still tender,
> and an only child of my mother,

he taught me, and said,
> "Take hold of my words with all your heart;
> keep my commands, and you will live.

Get wisdom, get understanding;
> do not forget my words or swerve from
> them.

Do not forsake wisdom, and she will protect you;
> love her, and she will watch over you.

Wisdom is supreme; therefore get wisdom.

## Understanding

Though it cost all you have, get understanding.
Cherish her, and she will exalt you;
>    embrace her, and she will honor you.
She will set a garland of grace on your head
>    and present you with a crown of splendor."
>              —Proverbs 4:1-9 (NIV)

# Source

## Go To The Source

The great American philosopher Deputy Barney Fife, summed it up so eloquently when he proclaimed, "Nip it! Just nip it in the bud!" Leadership requires you to confront problems head on, so, like Barney, nip them in the bud before the problems progress. If you want a leader's focus, go to the source with your problems and praise. Criticize people in private and praise people in public. Don't go around fussing and gossiping about someone. Go to the person involved, communicate openly, and solve the problem. Few people like to confront problems, but if you are not confronting and solving problems, you are not leading. I often think people who intentionally avoid confrontation are the biggest jerks of all, because when everything falls apart, they can throw their hands up and say, "But I'm a nice guy!" This, however, is just another way of saying I don't care. As mentioned earlier in the 5 H's of a leader, a cohesive team rallying around and working toward the top goal of the corporate body must be established. Where you are going is important, but just as important is "Who is going with you?" Don't be afraid to go to the source of the problem and, if need be, eliminate the source of the problem. Remember, a company is only as good as its worst employee.

I am often asked, "How do you motivate people around you?" The answer is really not complicated. Everyone wants to be praised, appreciated, needed, encouraged, challenged, and inspired to be better. You've heard it a thousand times, but the Golden Rule sums it up: Treat people the way you want to be treated. I once read of a study that was done in the 1950s, in which researchers surveyed more than 10,000 employees and asked what they wanted more of from their jobs. The supervisors were asked what they thought the employees would say; they assumed it would be more pay, benefits, time off, etc. However, overwhelmingly, the top things employees wanted most was to be praised, valued, and appreciated. The same study was conducted again 50 years later with the same results. People don't leave their jobs; they leave management. Ask yourself what you don't like about your job, and most likely, drama and politics will come to mind. Create an environment of encouragement and watch productivity soar. More gold has been mined from the brains of men and women than has ever been taken from the earth.

(Personal note: I have literally seen children and adults grow in stature as I was praising them. They were so deflated that even the smallest bit of encouragement made a visible and physical difference in their posture. Like an inflating ball, their chests stuck out, their eyes opened wider, and smiles instantly formed. No cliché intended—many even had a bounce in their step.)

When you go to the source, keep in mind to be specific, frequent, and genuine with your praise. The worst thing you can do is to just say, "You're doing a good job." Be specific or you will leave the impression you are disconnected or have no idea what they have done. Praise people in public, openly, honestly, and often. How do you know if someone needs encouragement? If they're breathing. Find something good to say about the people you interact with and do it as often as you can. Keep in mind, people know a fake. If you're not going to do it with sincerity, don't do it at all.

## Consider The Source

Michael Broome, in his bestseller Be a Liver of Life, Not a Gall Bladder, records this tale: Wilma Raghead was an inspector of wax fruit at the local wax fruit factory. As the inspector, she loved to criticize the work of her fellow employees. On the day of the factory's annual Wax Fruit Banquet, the workers arranged a special display of their fruit for the evening's festivities. A new employee who had yet to experience Wilma's negative critical tongue mistakenly asked her opinion of their display.

Suddenly, a hush fell over the crowd as all eyes and ears were upon Wilma. She jumped at this opportunity to demonstrate her superior knowledge by belittling their wax fruit. She mocked the curvature of their bananas. She smirked at the lack of fuzz on their peaches. She further noted that their grapes were anemic and their prunes were—irregular.

As she continued her critique, the crowd began to laugh and snicker at Wilma. Shocked, she realized why. The fruit she had criticized was not made of wax—it was actually real. The moral of this story is always be careful when you criticize the fruit of others' labor.

I truly believe there are people in this world who wake up and say to themselves, "How can I make other people's lives miserable?" The kind of people that when they leave, the room brightens up! You feel wrinkly like a raisin around these people because they have sucked the life out of you. Understand if you want to live a leader's focus, you must step outside the bounds of mediocrity. Unfortunately, the price you must pay for stepping outside the norm, the average, the status quo, is criticism. Always consider the source of the criticism to determine whether your focus is on track.

One Christmas, I received a spy novel as a gift. The only thing I can remember from the book was what an agent said to a young recruit, who was learning how to disguise himself in a crowd using big hats and dark glasses and a fake mustache. The old agent laughed at the young, naive recruit and simply said, "If you want to disappear . . . be ordinary. Ordinary is invisible." That simple quote applies to all walks of life and is used every day to get our attention in marketing campaigns.

If you want to be invisible, be ordinary. If you do not want to live an ordinary, common, average life, be prepared to be criticized for such actions. A note of caution: There is, of course, a sense of balance that needs to be considered in that statement. Many people feel that in order to be "different" or "non-conformist," they must mutilate themselves into a human pincushion, or wear their clothes a certain way, or always stretch the boundaries of morality. This behavior is not what I am condoning. Oddly enough, it is the "non-conformists" who are the most conforming; it is their underlying need to be accepted that induces this behavior. Rather than discovering and developing their own unique talents and abilities, they conform to the masses only to become invisible. You only need to have written goals and a plan to be in the top three percent of the U.S. You only need to live within your means to live differently than 75 percent of America. To have loving and open communication with your spouse will make you different than half of U.S. marriages. Watch out—if you eat more than four meals a week with your entire family, you're radical!

The point of "consider the source" is that when you step outside the bounds of mediocrity and "normal" thought patterns, you will be criticized, but always consider the source of that criticism. If someone is there to build themselves up while tearing you down, forgive and forget them. If you can't avoid them, kill them with kindness.

When you place a number of crabs in a bucket, there is always one that will try to climb out, but undoubtedly, the mass of crabs below will pull the escaping crab back in and prevent it from reaching its goal. Likewise, don't allow unproductive criticism to fill your mind, pull you down, and hinder you from your goals. Don't listen to people who tell you no who have no power to tell you yes. However, if a friend— someone who is genuinely happy for your success— criticizes you, think about what they have said and make appropriate changes. Always be willing to accept and be open to criticism.

Unfortunately, negative criticism tends to stick more in our heads and can often linger for years.

I can remember speaking to a group and afterward receiving their evaluations of the presentation. Every single evaluation was extremely positive and quite humbling. Everyone except . . . yes, one negative review. I don't know if this person was having a bad day. It may have even been a joke, but now, more than ten years later, I have forgotten the positive notes and still remember, word for word, the unflattering review. It is so important you consider the source of criticism and not allow it to fester into doubt. I use that review now as part of a joke in one of my stories, so honestly, I'm now thankful I received it because it brings a good laugh.

Special note to the criticizer out there: What goes in is what comes out. In other words, the words you say are often a reflection of your soul. (Unfortunately, you may only be replaying the tapes that were recorded into you years ago. For that, I am deeply sorry and pray that those words that were planted in you stop with you.)

It is physically and emotionally impossible to push someone down while building yourself up. The only way you can continue to push others down is by going down as well.

> Nowhere in history or in the world today is there a monument, memorial, or sanctuary to a critic.

If you want to destroy your organization, school, church, or company, continue to give and allow unproductive criticism. It only takes a spark to make a fire, and weeds start with a seed. Once again, "Nip it in the bud!"

Proverbs 27:5-6 says, "Faithful are the wounds of a friend, but the kisses of an enemy are deceitful." Someone who will be honest and correct you is much better than the friend who says nothing for fear of hurting your feelings. So a true friend may hurt your feelings and appear to attack you, but that is far better than the enemy who lies and misguides you in an attempt to gain your trust.

"He who rebukes a man will in the end gain more favor than he who has a flattering tongue." —Proverbs 28:23

# Smile

A genuine smile from deep down inside is an outward expression of happiness from within. You want a good focus and balance in life? Give everyone you know a good hearty genuine smile.

## A Two-Hour Smile

With only minutes to spare, I ran to my flight. I had a speaking engagement in Florida and could not miss this connection. When I approached my gate, I was able to slow my stride and in doing that, I began noticing strange expressions on people's faces. A young couple passed and I heard one say, "Wow, did you see that guy? He looked terrible!" Another man passed grimacing. As I turned into the waiting area, I heard someone whisper, "I'm glad my kids aren't here. He would have given them nightmares!"

I didn't understand what the commotion was about until I looked up. To my horror, I saw a man so severely burned, I nearly gasped out loud. He had no hair on his head or eyebrows. His ears had been melted off, revealing only holes. You could barely distinguish his eyes. His nose was an open cavity. He stretched his lower lip over the area his upper lip would have covered, if he had had one. Because his skin was a patchwork of stretched skin grafts, you couldn't tell whether he was 80 or 18. His left arm stopped at his elbow and his right arm had four little digits that were actually toe grafts. Honestly, he looked like a monster, and I was hardly prepared.

Though his looks were shocking, it was the reaction of the crowd that shocked me more. My heart broke for this man. He stood isolated and completely alone against the wall. More than 100 people stood 20 feet away, unsuccessfully trying to hide their stares. I was there for only a second when the attendant started the boarding process, but I can remember sincerely praying, "God, if I had only been here a few minutes earlier, I could have talked to the man or at least stood beside him." However, the opportunity was lost as the man joined the boarding line and soon after made his way to the plane.

Watch out what you pray for, because you might just get it! When it was my turn to enter the plane, I found my seat, and to my surprise, the man was sitting beside me. I was not given a few minutes to stand beside him but two hours to sit and hear his story. His name was Paul, and he was 36 years old. At the age of two, he was in a car accident that burned more than 90 percent of his body. It was a miracle that he even survived. During our time together, we laughed and had one of the deepest, heartfelt conversations I had ever had with anyone in my life. As we began our descent, I mentioned I was going to speak at a convention of about 8,000 students. I asked him if he could give me one piece of wisdom that he wished people knew or would do. In almost a whisper, Paul said to me, "Every day of my life I hear that I am a monster. Every time I look in the mirror I see the image that horrifies children. But what I've discovered is, if you look past our 'earth suits,' we're all the same. Everyone wants the very thing I crave so badly. I want people to look at me . . . not what they see. Look me in the eye and smile at me. If people only knew how powerful a simple smile was . . . I wish people could look each other in the eye and see each other for who they really are."

Never underestimate the power of a heartfelt smile. Give every living soul you meet the best smile you've ever smiled in your life. Smile to strangers, co-workers, your spouse, and your children. Smile while you're on the phone, because it shines through in your voice. Smile and see how much better you feel and look. Watch how quickly relationships are built or mended and barriers are broken. I have instantly bonded with people because of their contagious smiles. Yes, you will find those who absolutely refuse to smile, but smile at them anyway. You never know what people are going through.

Smiling makes you more approachable, accepted, and real! Our world has gone through the industrial age and technological age and is now in the information age. Though we have an instant and infinite amount of information at our fingertips, we seem to be losing the art of starting, building, and maintaining relationships. Remember, the essence of any successful business, organization, church, or family is successful relationships. One of the simplest ways to start that all-too-important relationship is through a simple, genuine smile! Smiling is therefore a key component of a leader's focus.

# Self

"Let another man praise you, and not your own mouth; A stranger, and not your own lips."
—Proverbs 27:2, NKJV

"If you want to change the world, you must first change yourself." —Gandhi

## Faux-Real

When I was a young man I wanted a Rolex watch. I'm not sure why I liked them, but they looked nice and I knew they were a high-quality products. So I worked hard, saved my money, and had enough to one day buy a Rolex watch. Years later, I was standing on the sidewalk of Times Square in New York City, when a man wearing a long bulky jacket approached me. He stood fairly close, leaned in, and whispered, "Hey, you want to buy a watch?" Slightly interested, I said, "Sure. Whacha got?" With a quick survey of the scene, the man grabbed the edges of his jacket and flashed it open to reveal an assortment of hanging watches. He saw what caught my eye and pulled off a beautiful silver Rolex watch. "Listen, man, this watch normally cost about $35,000," he confided. "But! . . . You look like a nice guy . . . so for today, and today only . . . I'll sell it to you"—shifting his eyes— "for 20 bucks." I couldn't believe it! A Rolex watch for $20! This was a dream come true! I may be a redneck, but I'm no dummy! I knew this was a good deal! When it was all said and done, I had even haggled the man down for less. Can you believe I bought a $35,000 watch for $15! A Rolex watch for 15 dollars! I must have broken the poor man's spirit because he quickly zipped up shop and hurried away.

I finally had myself a Rolex watch! It looked like a Rolex, sounded like a Rolex, kept time like a Rolex, it even said it was a Rolex. But in truth, was it a Rolex? Of course not, it was so fake I called it a Folex! I didn't even take it off going through a metal detector. It looked like the real deal but inside, it was cheap, plastic junk.

I still wear the "Rolex" watch occasionally. It's a poignant reminder of what not to be. It's sad that it shares very similar characteristics with many people walking around. They look good, talk the talk, and "have everything," but on the inside they are falling apart. People want to be around people who are the real deal, so just be yourself. As my Grandma would often say, "Be who you is, and not who you ain't, cause if you is who you ain't, you ain't who you is."

How exhausting and futile it is to alter your life and behavior based on the comparison and opinion of others. We are so concerned by what others may think, we change who we are. How many people come to mind matching that description? Do people put *you* in that category? If you want a leader's focus, remember, it doesn't matter what other people think about you. What's important is what you truly think about yourself. You can never accept others until you have accepted yourself. The reality . . . You'll stop worrying about what other people think about you when you realize how much they don't.

In order to be productive, you have to focus on your specific talents and abilities. Focus on what you can do. Don't compare what you're doing to what others are doing or what you can't do. If you spent your time focused on and developing the things you can do, you'll be far too busy to worry about the things you can't do. Comparing yourself to others is a bottomless pit. Please don't misunderstand me—there are people we should learn from, model after, and even emulate at times. But you must be conscious of the balance between comparing yourself to others and being yourself. Improve who you are rather than try to be someone you're not.

# Law Abiding

Good, better, best, never let it rest, until your good is better and your better is your best.

If you observe others, you will find this statistic to be true: In every group of people, whether in a company, school, or church, you will find that 10 percent will be leaders or winners, 80 percent will be lookers or watchers, and the final 10 percent will be leaners or whiners. That means 10 percent will lead with vision, values, empathy, passion, encouragement, and motivation. If the winning leader says, "Let's go this way!" the leaners will whine and say, "Let's go the other way." As the struggle of leadership versus leanership takes place, the lookers watch for which one wins the battle and subsequently follow. I've learned in most circumstances that progressive or digressive actions are the results of energy exerted to create momentum. Momentum is a slow-moving train, but once it gets going, things start happening. If you can pull that 80 percent in your direction, you have a lot of force and power that can take on a life of its own.

A Leader's Focus is for the daring 10 percent who are leading and winning. But it is also to encourage the 80 percent to follow and learn to lead with a leader's focus. The remaining 10 percent are leaners and whiners. Leaners and whiners say: "You'll never amount to anything . . . It will never work . . . It's too risky . . . People have tried it before . . . You're out of your league . . . You're too old, too young, too fat, too skinny, too much melanin, not enough melanin, too dumb, too smart . . . Play it safe . . . You'll always be in debt . . . Freedom is a fairytale."

It takes energy to be hot or cold, and nothing but the least resistance to be lukewarm. Average is best of the worst and worst of the best. All throughout this book I emphasize the importance of a balanced life, and if there was something that contradicts the value of a balanced life, it would be the default to be average. When in human history has average been productive?

*US News and World Report* once studied 1,000 kindergarten students and asked each student to "Describe your life." More than 90 percent said positive and encouraging things like, "Life is great, wonderful, adventurous, and fun." The same students were tracked throughout school and then asked the same question when they reached the 12th grade. Out of those same students who overwhelmingly had a positive view of life, more than 80 percent now made remarks like, "Life sucks, it stinks, it's not fair, what's the point?" Like these students, the majority of us at some point have a strong and energetic outlook of life. We have goals and dreams but the forces of time, fear, and failure pull us to a state of life that settles for mediocrity: The Law of Least Resistance.

The Law of the Pendulum is similar. Imagine a rope is attached to the ceiling, and attached to the other end of the rope is a bowling ball. The ball is then pulled back toward you and held just to the tip of your nose. The ball is then released and swings out, reaches its maximum height, and then swings back toward your nose. If you remained motionless, would the ball hit you? According to physics and the Law of the Pendulum, no, it will not. The drag or friction on the ball and string slows the motion of the ball just enough that it will never return to the starting position without new energy exerted on it.

The Law of the Pendulum is an unfortunate portrayal of an average life. We are born with energy, excitement, imagination, and curiosity; however, as we swing through life, our energy finds drag due to failure, fear, criticism, and discouragement. Over a lifetime we slow to the point of equilibrium—no movement. Our lives will never improve until we are constantly changing and the energy that we exert is greater than the drag or resistance we encounter. The world is full of unused talent and latent abilities. The reason these talents lie buried is that the individual hasn't the courage to dig them up and use them. Everyone should be doing better than they are, but only a few dare to go against the norm.

People often fall into the trap of riding their accomplishments far too long without exerting new energy—that is, change, ideas, and goals. People and companies often achieve and then slowly plateau. The problem is that in life, there are no plateaus. You are either going up or going down. Use moving moments to help you push to a higher level. Do not ride the momentum so long that the ride stops.

# Recharge

One of the safety procedures heard on a commercial plane is "if oxygen masks are released, place the mask on yourself before you assist others in need." The first time I heard that instruction, I was a bit offended! I thought if something went wrong, I would first take care of my child before I took care of myself! However, I quickly realized I'm no use to anyone if I'm dead. I can't take care of my family and be productive in my career if I have not taken care of myself.

We live in a culture that pushes people to work, work, work. Does more activity really mean more accomplishments? Is productivity being un-available to friends and family, to miss the sunsets and the full moons, to move about fulfilling our obligations without time to smell the roses? When was the last time you walked to a flower and smelled its fragrance? Is your perpetual busyness the  model of a "successful" life? Remember, the busiest chicken in the farm yard is the one running around with its head cut off.

Take time for yourself to be the best you can be. Recharge your batteries. If God can rest after six days of hard work, then so should we. Studies have proven that a simple 20–30 minute nap after learning something can help with retention. In fact, those who had naps greatly outscored those who did not. When we rest, our minds actually process the information and order it for better retention and understanding.

So give yourself time to rest and recharge. Find that balance of working to live or living to work. You don't always have to "be productive." Life is like an epic race: you have to give yourself finish lines, or the constant going results in a total burnout, bringing down yourself, your business, and your relationships. Recharging is sleep, laughter, recreation, and spending time with your children. Remember, you can't take care of others until you have taken care of yourself.

## Selfishness

Dealing with thousands of crimes in his career, Lt. Leso from Spartanburg County Sheriff Department planted this seed in my mind: "Selfishness is the root of all evil." All wrongs, whether personal, corporate, or governmental, have selfishness at their roots. If selfishness is the root, you have no fruit. By default, selfishness equals loneliness and isolation because you are only thinking about and providing for yourself. Serving others, on the other hand, brings at least one other person into the equation, which provides the opportunity for a lasting and profitable relationship.

Everything in this book that we have discussed, encouraged, and promoted is rendered useless with this simple word: Selfishness. Selfishness will warp your priorities and will destroy your relationship with God, your spouse, your children, and your friends, and will decimate your desire to serve others. Selfishness will destroy your character, break communication, and steal your financial peace. It will cloud your ability to learn and teach because it will disguise itself in pride. Selfishness leads a person to be too insecure to praise others or confront problems; it simply emboldens the individual to focus on his or her namesake, the self. Selfishness is the antithesis of a leader's focus and the seed to your destruction.

When I balance objects on my chin, whether it's ladders, a boat, or a teenager, my eyes are constantly focused on one place. I cannot look away for even a second. Selfishness is the equivalent of my balancing two 10-foot ladders in the center of a crowd and then closing my eyes. Not only will the things I'm balancing fall apart, but they will also hurt or destroy those around me as well. You cannot—will not—sustain a leader's focus if selfishness is the motivator.

# ONE BRIGHT DAY

When I was a kid I loved going to my grandparents' house! I loved hearing my grandfather tell stories. He told us of his adventures as a kid, from hunting rabbits and skinny-dipping in the creek to playing chicken on power lines to fishing with dynamite and telephone cranks. Grandpa had adventures, and he passed that spirit down to his two sons, eight grandchildren, and now twenty-four great-grandkids (and growing). He would gather us around and tell us of his adventures and always close his tales with a silly little poem, saying, "Listen carefully, kids. I want to tell you something important! Don't miss the point, so listen up:

It all happened right here . . . far, far away.
A long time ago . . . just yesterday.

It was one bright day, in the middle of the
night,
Two dead soldiers got up to fight.
Back to back they faced each other,
Drew their swords and shot each other.
A deaf policeman heard the noise,
And got up to arrest the two dead boys.
Oh, if you don't believe this story is true,
Ask Charlie the blind man, he saw it too!

The little poem would always give us a laugh
although it made no sense. One day someone asked,
"Grandpa, why do you always tell us that silly little
poem? It's crazy and makes no sense!" I'll never forget that day when Grandpa looked us in the eyes and
said, "You know what's silly? You know what doesn't
make sense? You know what's really crazy? It's someone with goals, passion, and God-given talents and
they never use them to make a difference in this
world. That's what's crazy!" Grandpa always challenged us to live a life of purpose and significance.
Likewise, find your place and tell your story through
your God-given gifts and abilities.

# CONCLUSION

What separates those who live an exceptional life from those who live a life of existence? Success is something you attract by the person you become, because successful people do the things that unsuccessful people do not have the heart to do. Living an exceptional and successful life means acting on principles that have been handed down since the dawn of time. King Solomon had it right; there is nothing new under the sun. It doesn't matter how many times you hear a great principle; until you make the conscious choice to act on those principles, you will never change. Doing the same thing over and over but expecting different results is the definition of insanity!

George Washington Carver wrote, "No individual has any right to come into the world and go out of it without leaving behind him distinct and legitimate reasons for having passed through it." I believe it is our right, if not our obligation, to tell our story and find our place on this universal pebble we call Earth. There is an old, worn-out phrase, "The past is history, tomorrow is a mystery, that's why they call today the present." Life is truly a gift! Each day we wake up to live another day is a day that was not guaranteed to us.

This is it. It's over. My favorite part . . . it's time to GO. In sports and many occupations, you don't practice day in and day out just to practice. You don't train hour after hour just to train. No, you prepare yourself to GO on the field and play the game. So the choice is yours. We live and die by the choices we make and do not make. You can make your dream come alive or it can die with you. Go now and put your energy into becoming a better you, the best you. Tell your story and choose to live A Leader's FOCUS.

"There is nothing brilliant, nor outstanding in my re-cord, except perhaps this one thing: I do the things that I believe ought to be done . . . .And when I make up my mind to do a thing, I act."
—Theodore Roosevelt

We invite you to continue your experience with
A Leader's FOCUS
at our website:

Stories
That Tell...
TELLING STORIES THAT
EQUIP TODAY'S LEADERS

www.ALeadersFocus.com

- Share how you feel about A Leader's FOCUS and read what others are saying.
- Share your insights and discuss the book with other readers at the FOCUS Form.
- Communicate with Thomas.
- Read more of Thomas's short stories.
- Purchase additional copies of the A Leader's FOCUS.
- Find out the latest news on how YOU can tell YOUR story.

For information about having Thomas Dismukes speak to your group, please contact:
booking@storiesthattell.com

This book has had phenomenal success because of passionate readers who wanted to pass it along to their friends, family, students and coworkers. If you are taken with the message of this book as we are, you may already have some unique ideas as to how you can best let others know about it. If you'd like to share this book with others, here are some ideas to help others have A Leader's FOCUS.

Give the book to friends, even strangers, as a gift. They not only get great little stories but also tools that will help as a guide in life.

If you have a website or blog, consider sharing a bit about the book and how it has touched your life. Recommend that they read it as well and link to www.ALeadersFocus.com.

Write a book review for your local paper, favorite magazine, or website you frequent. Ask your favorite radio show or podcast to have Mr. Dismukes on as a guest. The media often gives more consideration to the request of their listeners than the press releases of publicists.

If you own a shop or business, consider putting a display of these books on your counter to resell or give away to customers. We make books available at a discounted rate for resale. For individuals we offer volume discount pricing for orders of a dozen books or more.

Buy a set of books as gifts to students, family, coworkers, employees, leadership and continuing education conferences, retreats, prisons, and others who will be really encouraged by A Leader's FOCUS and its message.

Talk about the book on e-mail lists you are on, forums you frequent, and other places you engage people on the internet. Don't make it an advertisement, but share how this book impacted your life and offer people the link to A Leader's FOCUS site.

Thank you again and again for your
continued support!

# What's YOUR Story?

For more up-to-date information and ideas of how
you can help and have the opportunity to participate
in Stories That YOU Tell, please check out
YOUR STORY at:
www.StoriesThatTell.com

# About the Author

Thomas Dismukes' appeal is universal. Since 1991, more than a million people across the U.S. and 19 countries have heard his unbelievable but true stories.

Receiving a master's degree from Clemson University, Thomas chose a career in professional speaking because of his sincere passion to inspire people to do their best and get the best out of life. His purpose is to encourage others to discover, develop, and tell *their* story through their unique talents and gifts.

Never turning down an opportunity for a good story or a miserable time, Thomas's true life adventures range from sleeping in dumpsters in England to exploring the Arctic Circle. He's survived bareback rodeos, skunks in space suits and electrocution in Sweden. He's walked through the Alps barefoot, and discovered a lost medieval tomb in Scotland. He's lassoed a wild beaver, broken a World Record and was nearly drowned by an irrational goose.

Thomas has a unique ability to discern a meaning behind the madness in a principle everyone can relate to, laugh at, and apply to their lives. Thomas lives in the heart of the Tennessee Appalachian Mountains but owns a farm in South Carolina just in case the world comes to an end.

CPSIA information can be obtained at www.ICGtesting.com
Printed in the USA
LVOW07s0022220814

400301LV00001B/1/P